"To my wife Kath. When I told her I was going to write another book her eyes rolled skywards and she grimaced. Anyone would think it was going to take months and months. How right she was! Many thanks for your patience. I promise I will now get on with the items on the Things to Do list left over from the previous book."

ADDING SPICE
TO YOUR WOODTURNING
20 Salt, Pepper & Spice Shaker Projects for Woodturners

Chris West

ADDING SPICE
TO YOUR WOODTURNING

20 Salt, Pepper & Spice Shaker Projects
for Woodturners

ARTISAN
IDEAS

Published by Artisan Ideas.
Text by Chris West.
ISBN 978-0-9979798-0-0, First Edition.
Library of Congress Control Number: 2016952602
Printed in China.
Artisan Ideas is an imprint of Artisan North America.
Copyright © 2017 by Artisan North America, Inc.
Tel: 800-843-9567, Fax: 717-724 3015
Info@ArtisanIdeas.com
www.ArtisanIdeas.com

Artisan North America
753 Valley Road
Watchung, NJ 07069-6120

Ordering Information:
Quantity sales. Special discounts are available on quantity purchases by corporations,
associations, and others. For details, contact the publisher at the address above.
For single copies, please try your bookstore first. If unavailable this book can be ordered
through: www.ArtisanIdeas.com.
To see our complete selection of books and DVDs on this and related subjects visit
our website listed above.

Authors!
If you have an idea for a book please contact us at: Info@ArtisanIdeas.com.
We'll be glad to hear from you.

INTRODUCTION

Salt and pepper shakers are often considered the poor relations among woodturners. It's mills and grinders that steal the scene and are most often seen in woodturning magazines and books. This project book tries to address this injustice by offering the reader 15 different salt and pepper shaker projects!

Shakers on dining tables are usually run-of-the-mill glass or white ceramic containers which are unmemorable. An attractive hand turned wooden shaker, on the other hand, gives an excellent impression.

You may be making these shakers as gifts for friends and family or simply to give your own kitchen an extra touch, but well-crafted shakers are also easily sold in markets and through your website. However, as I know to my cost, if you are selling your work to restaurants, an attractive shaker does leave itself open to being kept by the customer as a souvenir.

In addition, this book goes one step further and introduces a bonus section that has several projects including 3 genuine spice shakers. While you will find glass or tin containers in kitchen cupboards containing spices such as mixed herbs, cinnamon, cayenne, fennel seeds, etc., you will not often see these spices contained in a wooden shaker.

The main technical problem is the necessary 'air-tight lid', which is rarely seen on a wooden shaker. With this in mind, the spice shaker projects were introduced to show ways to address this issue. Hopefully you will learn a trick or two.

The objective of this book is NOT to teach you how to turn; there are numerous excellent books already available on this subject. Rather, it was written to allow those who already have a knowledge of basic wood-turning to get right down to the projects themselves without needing to read through introductory material they are familiar with.

The aim is to offer the reader some straightforward, easily understandable

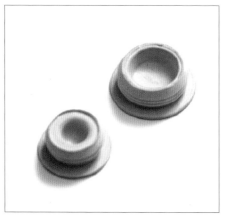

Bungs

Chrome cap

technical information which will give the knowledge to help them turn the projects and design their own shakers.

Each of the projects has a rating of beginners, intermediate or experienced and is presented on two facing pages. The book is designed to stand up to workshop use. It is hardcover and is also spiral bound to allow facing pages to lie flat on the workbench. The pages are heavy-duty art paper.

I have tried to eliminate the need for specialist tools to allow all woodturners, regardless of their budget, to be able to turn any of the projects.

When I started out with this book I had made a conscious effort not to get involved in the argument/discussion on the size and number of holes a salt or pepper shaker should have. Let's get this straight, there is no written rule!

In the USA, pepper is often found in the shaker with a single hole and salt in shakers with multiple holes. In the UK it is the opposite.

So here we go; throughout this book I am going to go with the UK rule. Salt has one hole and pepper more. The size of the hole will be $\frac{1}{16}$ in (2 mm) diameter.

My reasoning is the following: the UK public is told that an adult's daily salt intake should be kept down to one teaspoon, 0.2 oz (6 g). Based on this, one hole in my salt shaker should help limit the amount I put on my food as long as I also reduce the number of shakes I give it!

Please feel free to reverse this and/or change the size of the holes. The key thing is to clearly identify to the user which shaker contains what.

The accessories needed for a pair of shakers are usually just a bung and a salt cap or a screw cap and a cylindrical container.
Inexpensive for such a lovely gift.

Salt caps and cylinders

A1. HEALTH AND SAFETY

Introduction

Common sense – that's what Health and Safety is all about. Using a lathe and associated accessories is all about taking your time and *thinking* before doing something. It is described in the Collins dictionary as the *"natural ability to make good judgments and behave sensibly."*

While most of the points detailed below are obvious, you will find a number which derive from experience, so please take a few minutes to read on. It may well make a difference to how long you get to enjoy woodturning.

A woodturner, dressed sensibly, ready for action with a modern full-face helmet with respirator.

Before starting the lathe

▲ Don't Drink and Turn.

▲ Wear safety glasses that include side protectors, or better still, a fullface shield.

▲ Ensure that nothing is hanging loose from you before starting the lathe. Loose sleeves, ties, long hair and jewellery can catch when the lathe is in motion.

▲ Consider purchasing a smock with elastic cuffs and a collar that zips to the neck. This will protect your clothes and stop shavings going into your shirt or upper clothing. A bonus will be that shavings don't get dropped on the bedroom floor which is a sure-fired way of upsetting the other half!

▲ Wear strong shoes, a falling skew chisel is not a good alternative to a pedicure!

▲ Ensure you have good lighting in your workshop.

▲ In dusty work conditions, use a dust mask or helmet, and a proper ventilation and dust-collection system.

▲ Check that the jaws can't fall out of the chuck.

▲ Before mounting the wood on the lathe, examine it carefully for splits and cracks. Be aware of any bark and/or knots that are present (avoid these altogether if you are inexperienced), and take into consideration any irregularities in the shape of the wood.

▲ Ensure that the tool rest is firmly locked in place.

▲ Rotate the piece by hand to ensure that it is running clear of the tool rest and bed.

▲ Ensure that you have no distractions, especially sudden ones like someone coming into your view unexpectedly.

▲ Be aware that certain woods may cause skin irritation in some individuals.

When turning

▲ Always use the tailstock when possible to steady the work.

▲ Always start a new piece at a slow speed until the wood is in balance.

▲ Stop the lathe and check if you detect strange sounds or vibrations, or anything that does not seem right to you. You know the sounds of your car; learn the sounds of your lathe.

▲ Sand the wood when it is turning towards you.

▲ Always use paper towels or a safety cloth when applying finishes; any other fabric could drag your hand into the work if it catches.

▲ Never leave your chuck key in the chuck.

▲ Never leave the lathe running unattended. Turn it off.

▲ Remember that dust and shavings are a potential fire hazard.

A2. WOOD

A number of questions arise when choosing your wood and a little time spent on this could well enhance the design and quality of your project. When I receive commissions for a pair of shakers, the client rarely has a clear idea of what wood to choose.

The choice of woods available to you nowadays is extensive. Are you going to leave the shaker natural? Is it to be oiled, sprayed with an acrylic finish, receive coats of a polyurethane finish or be colored? Knowing what finish you are going to use will help in your choice.

Whichever wood you choose it must be dry. If not the finished shaker can warp and the tenon will jam inside the main body making it unusable.

Try to avoid wood which has large knots in it unless you feel that the knot will enhance the end result. Branch wood can be turned into shakers but I would suggest that the pith should be in the center allowing it to be drilled out.

Since we are making items associated with food it is essential to avoid woods considered to be toxic. Also many woods cause adverse reactions with turners either in the form of external irritation or internal problems.

One type wood I have used in a project is yew. Despite the fact that the living tree is toxic and that the leaves and berries are poisonous, I have not found any evidence that the dry wood maintains these properties and should not be used for shakers. But to err on the side of caution you may feel that it is wise to wear a face mask when turning and sanding yew in exactly the same way you would with any timber

I have also used spalted beech. Spalting is part of the decay process and is caused by a fungus which attacks the tree. Dust particles from the wood contain the spores of the fungus which can affect the respiratory system, but the wood itself is unlikely to cause problems. Most commercially available salt and pepper shakers do not have a layer finish on the reservoir. If you are worried about this, consider lining the reservoir with a plastic tube.

Alternatively, coat the inside with a barrier or a certified salad bowl finish. Certification for food safe finishes varies from country to country, but will be clearly labelled as food or toy safe.

All wood produces fine particles of dust so, regardless of what wood you are using, good ventilation, dust extraction and face masks must be considered an integral part of your workshop.

Below are details of some of the woods I have used in projects. Unless otherwise stated, they all turn well and a good finish can be obtained if the correct finishing process is followed. There are many woods not listed which would be equally suitable.

It's worth finding out about those which are native to your own country.

Ash (American, Fraxinus Americana and European, Fraxinus excelsior)

European ash is an open grained wood that I use when ebonizing and gilding. Creamy in color, it can often be found to have areas of brown in it. European ash has a more wavy grain pattern than its American cousin which has a more yellowish/greenish tinge to it. It is also softer to turn than European ash. Origin: Ash is found throughout Europe, North America and Asia.

Maple, Acer saccharum

The color of maple ranges from nearly white to a cream color. Birdseye maple is a figure found most commonly in Hard maple. It turns and finishes well. Origin: Canada and North America.

Satiné bloodwood, Brosimum paraense

Also known as satiné because of its high lustre when finished. It is a very dense and hard wood with a tight grain. It is bright red and is the nearest I know to blood red! Origin: Brazil, Panama, Peru and Venezuela.

Yew, Taxus baccata

Boxwood, Buxus sempervirens

A heavy, hard and very fine grained wood, which is usually white or creamy in color. Variations of the Buxus family can be found around the world. I sometimes use it as a contrasting insert for the identification of a salt shaker. Origin: Europe and North America.

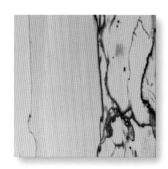

Bubinga, Guibourtia demeusei

It can vary from a pinkish red to a reddish brown heartwood. It's easy to work and finishes well. Origin: Africa and South America.

Cherry (American, Prunus serotina and European, Prunus avium)

Has quite a tight grain, is orange in color, which turns darker over time. European cherry has a more wavy grain than American cherry. They both turn well. Origin: throughout Europe and North America

Ebony, Diospyros crassiflora

A hard, tight, grained wood renowned for its finishing capabilities. Black in color, sometimes found with brown stripes. When turning it can be brittle, sharp tools are required. Origin: Western Africa.

European Oak, Quercus robur

Oak has an open texture and can be found in varying shades of brown. It darkens with age and has a lovely patina.
Looks attractive when limed. Origin: Europe and North Eastern areas of the USA.

Spalted beech, Fagus sylvatica

Spalted beech, Fagus sylvatica

It is a dense hard wood with an even grain. Spalting Is a discoloration caused by fungal attack. It is the first stage in decay, and sometimes the wood can become soft or rotten. No two pieces are the same. Origin: UK, Central Europe, West Asia.

Yew, Taxus baccata

Yew is reddish brown in color, which in time turns to a lovely orange/brown. Has a tendency to create crack lines if the lathe is running too fast while sanding. Origin: UK, Europe and North America.

A3. TURNING TOOLS

The tools shown below are the basic tools used in the projects in this book.

¾ in (19 mm)
Spindle Roughing Gouge

For the initial turning of uneven or square spindle stock to round.

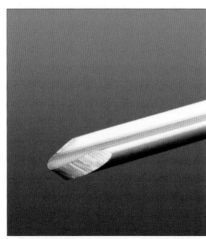

¼ in (6 mm)
Spindle Gouges

Detailing tools used on between-center-work where the grain is running parallel to the lathe.

½ in (12 mm)
Parting & Beading Tool

A versatile tool used for parting off as well as producing beads. Ideal for creating spigots and tenons to fit a chuck.

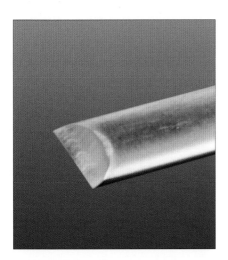

½ in (12 mm)
Skew Chisel

A tool that planes the wood. Also used for creating beads and dovetails.

³⁄₁₆ in (5 mm)
Fluted Parting Tool

This tool has a flute running along the bottom edge creating two sharp spurs at the cutting face. These sever the fibres to produce a burnished finish.

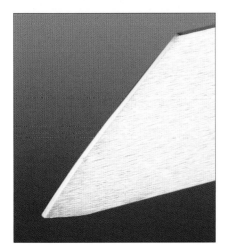

⅛ in (3 mm)
Parting Tool

Used to part the finished item from the waste wood. The parallel sides make for a rigid tool.

A4. FINISHING METHODS

Three things make an attractive piece of turning: the shape, the wood and the finish. Shakers receive a good deal of handling, so they need a durable finish.

Time spent on finishing will make the difference between your shaker being so-so and looking and feeling wonderful. In my opinion, finishing begins with the last cut with the gouge or skew chisel.

Sanding

The choice of a sanding paper is a personal thing. Cloth-backed aluminium oxide paper serves me well for most of my sanding needs.

With most woods I start with 120-grit paper and work my way to 400-grit. On smooth surfaces, I take the opportunity to stop the lathe after each grit and sand horizontally with the grain. Throughout the sanding process always reduce the lathe's speed to around 500 rpm.

Cellulose sealer

The basis of a waterproof finish is cellulose sealer. It is best applied by either a brush or with a safety cloth and will dry very quickly. I usually apply one coat which should be sufficient to fill the pores of the wood and form the base for a lacquer. After the sealer and before any further finishing product is applied, rub over the rotating shaker with a white synthetic finishing pad to remove any 'nibs' of sealer.

Defects and the use of CA, Superglue, Cyanoacrylates

You will occasionally find that a particularly attractive piece of wood you wish to use has small cracks; yew is prone to these. Superglue (cyanoacrylate) can be used to fill the cracks.

It comes in three consistencies: thin, medium and thick. Most times the thin or the medium will be suitable, depending on the size of the void to be filled. The hole or crack is first filled with matching wood dust and then the superglue. Once dry, the crack is hand-sanded to start with, before sanding with the lathe.

Oil

Oily woods such as rosewood and olive lend themselves to an oiled finish. Both Danish and finishing oil are suitable, but patience is required for any oil application.

If possible, leave the oiling process until the end of the day and allow to dry overnight. De-nib the surface between further coats.

Leave the piece for at least a week before progressing to the buffing process.

Spraying

All of my non-oily woods receive several coats of cellulose gloss lacquer. When I can't do this outdoors, I spray away from the lathe in a dust-free and well-ventilated area of the workshop.

Cellulose lacquer will dry in 20 minutes, depending on the ambient temperature. I recommend that the turned parts are put back on the lathe when dry to receive a de-nibbing between coats. The end result will be well worth the extra time. Usually a maximum of three coats will suffice.

I like to leave the sprayed items overnight before beginning the buffing process. I find that this 'hardening' time gives me a better end result than buffing immediately.

Buffing

All of my shakers receive the buffing process. I have three 6 in (150 mm) loose-stitched mops, which I mount individually on a right-hand-threaded polishing mop adapter held in chuck jaws. An alternative is to purchase a Beall polishing system, which comes with everything you will need to buff any wooden item.

The first mop, a sewn mop, is lightly loaded with tripoli, which is a gentle abrasive compound that will remove minor scratches. I should stress that this is not for removing scratch marks from a poor or rushed sanding job! The abrasive will not remove 120 grit sanding marks. The second mop, a different sewn mop, contains White Diamond, a micro-abrasive polishing compound, which removes traces of tripoli and creates a deep shine. Do not press the shaker too hard against the mop or 'smearing' will appear on the polished surface.

The third and final mop, a loose mop, is for applying a paste wax which is a blend of beeswax and carnauba wax. Apply a small amount and buff to create a final polish. Recently, as an alternative, I have been applying by hand micro crystalline Renaissance wax, a product developed for objects in the British Museum. The benefit of this wax is that it makes the piece waterproof and it does not show fingerprints. What you are trying to avoid is sticky-fingered users leaving permanent marks on your beautiful turned condiment shakers!

A5. DRILLS USED

Forstner *Sawtooth bits* are used to bore the holes for the bungs and reservoirs.

Also known as multi-spur sawtooth bits, they do need to be regularly sharpened to reduce overheating and to give a cleaner cut. They work well in end-grain, cut faster and, as long as the center point of the bit is sharpened correctly and in contact with the wood, they cut well. For the rest of this book I will be referring to these drilling bits as Sawtooth.

Fig A5-1 Sawtooth bit with masking tape marked to indicate depth required.

The two common sizes used in the projects are: ¾ in (19 mm) and 1 in (25 mm)

Sharpening sawtooth bits

Maintaining sharp edges on your bits is important. Frequent touching up on the cutting edges is recommended. It is easier to keep the original angles and edges if sharpening is frequent.

For the purpose of being able to sharpen all parts of the cutting surfaces 'fine' grade triangular diamond files are recommended, *Fig A5-2*.

Fig A5-2 A 'fine' graded triangular diamond file

The ideal speed the lathe should be running at when using sawtooth bits is 450-500 rpm. For holes smaller than ½ in (13 mm) twist drills are used.

Twist drills

The only twist drills I use for the projects are a ¹⁄₁₆ in (2 mm) and a ¼ in (6 mm) bit for some of the exit holes.

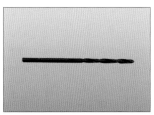

Shown is a ¹⁄₁₆ in (2 mm) engineering twist drill bit
These are used in the salt & pepper shaker projects to drill the exit holes for the salt or pepper.

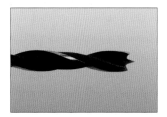

Shown is a ¼ in (6 mm) lip and spur bit, also known as a brad point drill or dowelling jig drill
The center point of this drill bit finds the center point more easily and is less inclined to wander as it progresses through the wood.

A6. TERMINOLOGY AND TURNING NOTES

The following specialist terms are used throughout this book:

Chuck expansion and compression mode
(see photo and caption)

Ø - This symbol is used on most of the project drawings to indicate that the dimension is the diameter.

Drive plug - Refers to the small component which can be slid into a shaker's reservoir.

Forstner v Sawtooth drill bits
The Forstner bit's rim gives it the ability to drill overlapping holes well, while the Sawtooth bit will give a clean hole especially into end-grain. In the US the sawtooth bit is often referred to as a Forstner.

Compression mode   Expansion mode

A woodturner should stick to sawtooth bits when drilling end-grain shakers.

Reservoir
The drilled hole within the body of the shaker that contains the salt or pepper.

*Throughout the projects I will be referring to the use of a chuck in **expansion mode** or **compression mode**. The photo gives a visual indication of this.*

Spigot and Tenon
An observation I have made while watching professional woodturners demonstrate both here in the UK and in the United States is that they use the words *Spigot* and *Tenon* to describe the same thing. A dictionary describes the use of these two words as:

Tenon: "a projection on the end of a piece of wood for insertion into a mortise".
Spigot: "a short projection on a component designed to fit into a hole or slot in a mating part"

There is little or no difference between the two, given these definitions. I have decided to use my own definitions for these two words which will apply throughout this book. They are:

Where a projection is being used as a means of holding a piece of wood in chuck jaws and will be eventually removed as waste wood, this is known as a SPIGOT.
Where a projection is being used as an integral part of a turned object and will be there on completion whether seen or not, then this is a TENON.

White PVA glue
Also know as Carpenter's glue.

A7. SHAKER ACCESSORIES

Bungs

The first thing we often associate with salt and pepper shakers is the bung in the base. The number of sizes available is considerable but with this book's projects you only need to be concerned with ¾ in and 1 in bungs.

Fig A7-1
Rubber bungs

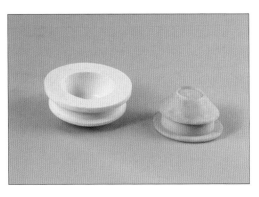

Hint:
I would recommend that you test out on a scrap piece of wood the diameter of the hole required for your bung. It should either be ¾ in or 1 in diameter, but can vary.

NOTE: if you find that you don't have the bung size shown in a project drawing, use a different size. With all things being equal and if there is enough wood to fit a different bung, go ahead.

If you want to design your own shaker which utilizes a different diameter bung to those above, the suppliers section on Page 66 lists bung providers that have all sizes available.

If you wish you could incorporate a wooden screw at the bottom. I do think however that this exposes the shaker to the problem of the salt getting between the threads and causing wear and tear and even tightness when unscrewing the thread.

Salt and pepper chrome caps

These are available from woodturning retailers. They alleviate the problem of drilling accurate holes for the condiments. *Fig A7-2* shows examples of commercially available chrome salt/pepper caps. Project 5 is an example of a shaker which uses a chrome cap.

Fig A7-2
Left - small ¹³⁄₁₆ in (21 mm) chrome salt/pepper cap.
Right - large 1⅜ in (35 mm) salt/pepper cap

Threaded salt cap and plastic cylinder containers

These make turning shakers very easy. They require a 1 in (25 mm) diameter hole, 2⅛ in (54 mm) deep. The container is held in place with silicone. Projects 1 and 2 use these cylinders.

If you do not have a suitable set of chuck jaws to hold the base of a shaker then a drive plug similar to that shown in *Fig A8-10* will do the job.

Fig A7-3 Set of threaded salt and pepper cylindrical containers

Silicone sealing ring

The silicone sealing ring is used to give an air-tight seal to the spice shakers.
Projects 16, 17 and 18 use this silicone ring.

Fig A7-4 Silicone sealing ring

A8. SHAKER JIGS

Which is the salt and which is the pepper shaker?
As mentioned in the book's Introduction I have made my rules which can be changed to suit your wishes.
A salt shaker has a single exit hole - a pepper shaker has more than one.
Having the letters S & P on each shaker gives a strong indication of the contents, although this method is not used in this book's projects.

1. The number of exit holes in the top of a shaker is a common method of identifying which is which.
2. The use of different looking inserts in the top of the shaker, see *Fig A8-3* below, is another.
3. The shaker can be made out of two different kinds woods. If the top half has a light colored wood and the bottom half a dark colored wood it identifies the shaker's contents as salt. When the reverse is used then the content is pepper.

*Fig A8-1
Drilling positions.*

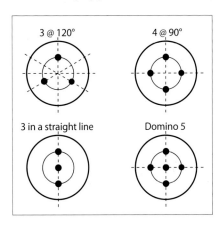

Number of holes and their placement

The number of and the positions of the exit holes for the pepper are your choice.
Here are four options.
Shown are just four of the many arrangements for drilling the exit holes for a pepper shaker. Why not design your own?

Options for drilling the exit holes for your shakers

1. Using a twist drill in a Jacobs chuck in the tailstock

For a salt shaker a single central hole can be drilled either while it is on the lathe or on a drill press.
Shown is the insert for the Beehive salt shaker having its salt exit hole drilled with a 1/16 in (2 mm) engineering twist drill.
The twist drill is held in a Jacobs chuck, which in turn is in the barrel of the tailstock.

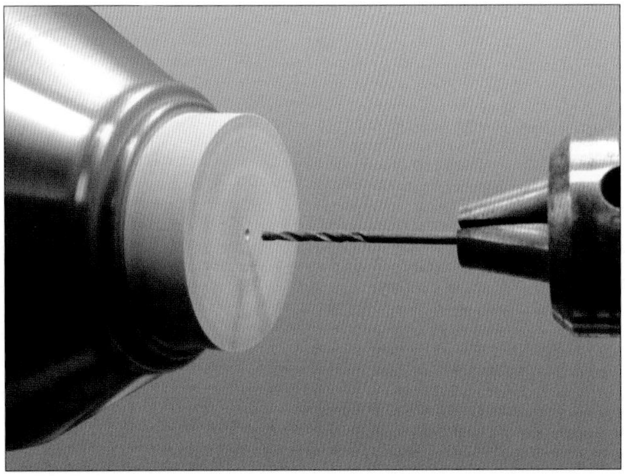

Fig A8-2. An example of this is project 14, Beehive shaker.

2. Holes can be 'eyeballed' to drill the exit holes.

The position of the exit holes can literally be 'eyeballed', punched with a center punch and drilled on a drill press.

3. Wood inserts

Fig A8-3

Inserts are primarily included to indicate the contents of the shaker. A light colored insert equating to salt and a dark wood to pepper, *Fig A8-3*. The number of exit holes is also an indication of the contents. They are usually drilled using a ¹⁄₁₆ in (2 mm) engineering twist drill.

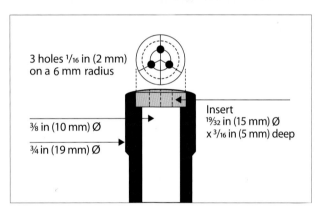

3 holes ¹⁄₁₆ in (2 mm) on a 6 mm radius

Insert ¹⁹⁄₃₂ in (15 mm) Ø x ³⁄₁₆ in (5 mm) deep

³⁄₈ in (10 mm) Ø

³⁄₄ in (19 mm) Ø

Fig A8-4
The drawing shows an example of the relationship between an insert and the top of the shaker.

Drilling accurately placed exit holes in an insert for a pepper shaker.

Draw on a piece of paper the diameter of the insert.
The holes are then positioned on the paper depending on the size of the insert and the reservoir hole it will sit over.
The paper template is either glued onto the top of the shaker or it is held over the insert with clear tape.
The hole positions are then center punched and drilled on a drill press using a ¹⁄₁₆ in (2 mm) engineering twist drill either held directly in a Jacobs chuck or a pin vice chuck.

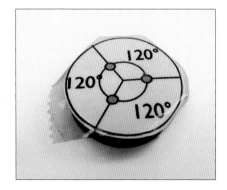

Fig A8-5

Finally the insert is sealed with sanding sealer and glued into the top of the shaker.
Align the insert's grain to that of the shaker. Lacquer and buff after allowing to dry overnight. A project example of this is the *Shap shaker*.

Insert Drilling Jigs

A drilling jig is placed over the top of a shaker top to line up the position of the holes to be drilled.

Projects which use this are the *Dufton shaker* and the *Tavy shaker*.

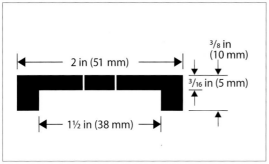

Fig A8-6

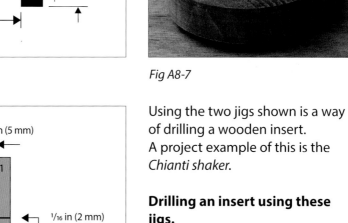

Fig A8-7

Using the two jigs shown is a way of drilling a wooden insert.
A project example of this is the *Chianti shaker*.

Drilling an insert using these jigs.

Turn the insert to the diameter you want or 1 in (25 mm) in this instance.
Part off at around ⁵⁄₁₆ in (8 mm) length.
Push the insert into Jig 2.
If it is a loose fit use a piece of paper towel to hold it firmly.
Face off the protruding insert to around ¼ in (6 mm) length.

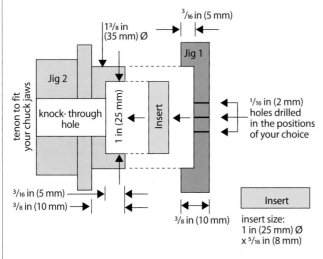

Fig A8-8

Remove the jig from the lathe with the insert still in place.
Place Jig 3 over it and proceed to drill the exit holes.
Drill the insert's recess hole in the top of the pepper shaker first, using a smaller drill.
Open up the shaker's recess hole to take the insert using the ½ in skew chisel, lying flat on its side.
When the drilling is completed, if the insert is tight in Jig 2, use a piece of dowelling to knock through the jig to remove the insert.
Glue in the insert and hold the shaker by its base and shape the top.

Pin Vice Drill Chuck

One way to hold the ¹⁄₁₆ in (2 mm) engineering twist drill is to use a pin vice drill chuck when your Jacobs chuck is too large to grip such a small drill. The pin chuck can be held in a drill press or in a Jacobs chuck in the tailstock of your lathe.

Fig A8-9
Pin chuck holding
a ¹⁄₁₆ in (2 mm)
twist drill.

Shaker turning Jigs

If you do not have a suitable set of chuck jaws which can hold and support the base of a shaker then a drive plug will do the job. *Fig A8-10*
Shown below is drive plug for supporting the bottom of a shaker while the top is shaped. The length of the shaft will differ between shakers.

Shaker support jigs, used for shaping the outside of the shaker.

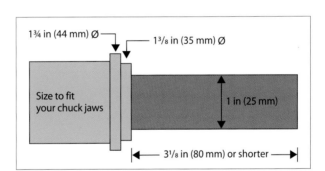

Fig A8-10

Fig A8-11 shows the support jig held in a chuck to support the bottom of a shaker when turning the outside shape. Dimensions for both jigs may well change to fit your chuck.

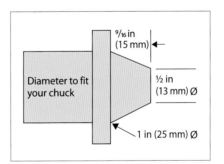

Fig A8-11

Where a live center is not suitable for whatever reason, a support jig for the top of a shaker when turning the outside shape can be used. The jig is supported by a live center in the tailstock.

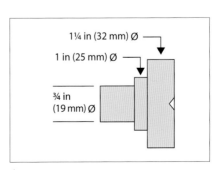

Fig A8-12

Dovetail

Spigot

Dovetail

Dovetail

C

B

Dovetail

Top tenon

A

C

B

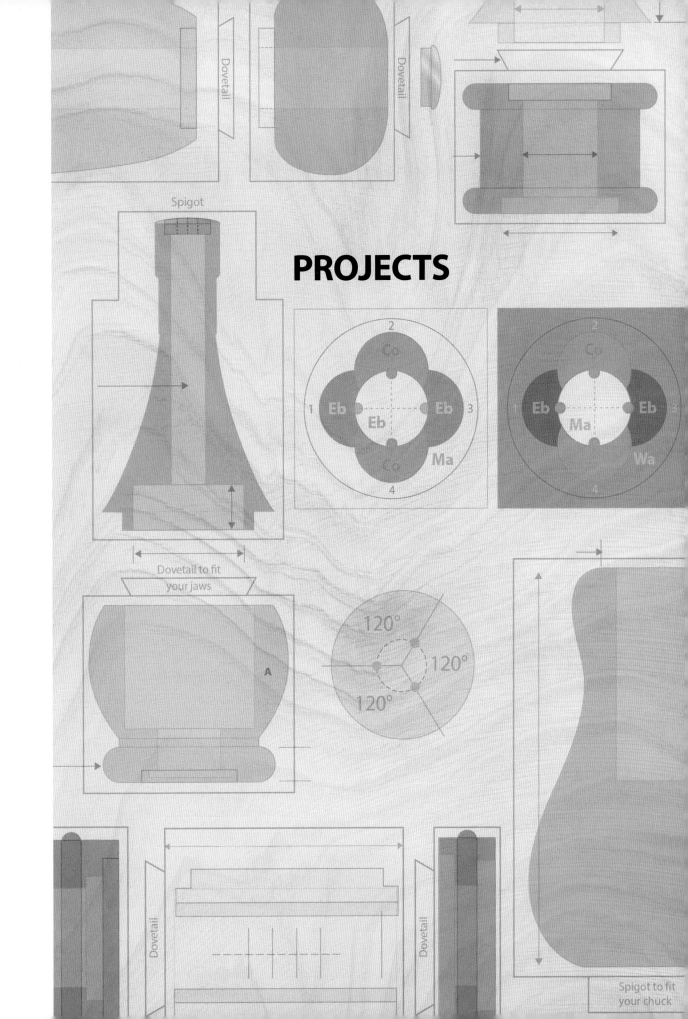

PROJECTS

1. APPLE

The first two projects, the Apple and Pear, have been designed so that you have a choice of making either a pair of apples or a pair of pears or one of each.

A drive plug is shown which will need to be turned. This is to support the apple while it is shaped and its base cleaned up.

The shaker shown was sanded to 400 grit and finished with a waterproof finish like finishing oil and then buffed.

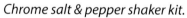
Chrome salt & pepper shaker kit.

An alternative to a pair of apples is an apple and pear (project 2).

Drilling and turning the shaker

Blank size: 3¼ x 3¼ x 3¼ in (83 x 83 x 83 mm)

Turn the blank with a spigot to fit your chuck jaws.
Hold by the spigot and face off the top of what will be the apple before drilling and forming the 1 in (25 mm) Ø x 2⅛ in (54 mm) deep hole for the container.
Shape the top of the apple, sand and seal. Remove from the lathe.
Reverse and in a chuck with compression jaws fit the drive plug below.
Slide the blank over it and once it is running true, measure and mark the overall height 2¾ in (70 mm).
Alternatively, hold the apple by its hole on expansion jaws in your chuck without the drive plug.
Part off at the marked line removing the spigot in the process. Shape the bottom half of the apple as shown.
The last part to be turned is the apple's base with a live center supporting the base, until the last minute.
This helps produce a nice clean cut and smooth base.

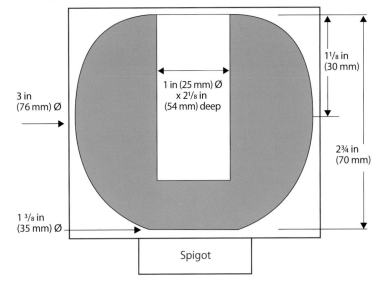

3 in (76 mm) Ø

1 in (25 mm) Ø x 2⅛ in (54 mm) deep

1⅛ in (30 mm)

2¾ in (70 mm)

1 ³/₈ in (35 mm) Ø

Spigot

Finally, sand, seal and finish.
Make the second shaker, whether it is to be another apple or a pear.
Because I was using 'cracked' yew I chose to dribble thin superglue (Cyanoacrylate) into the cracks before applying gold gilt cream.
After two hours I wiped the excess cream off with a piece of paper towel which had finishing oil on it.
Three further coats of finishing oil were applied before buffing.
The last task is to glue the salt and pepper containers into the shakers. Silicone sealant applied on the sides and at the base of the container will do the job.

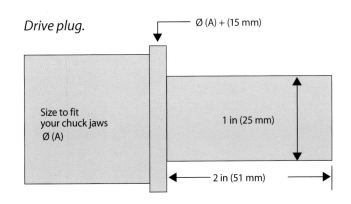

Drive plug.

Ø (A) + (15 mm)

Size to fit your chuck jaws Ø (A)

1 in (25 mm)

2 in (51 mm)

2. PEAR

The first two projects in this book were designed so that you have a choice of a pair of apples, a pair of pears or one of each; the apple for the salt and the pear for the pepper perhaps.

The drive plug shown in Project 1, Apple, will need to be turned. This is to support the pear while the bottom is turned.

The shaker should be sanded to 400 grit, finished with a waterproof finishing oil and buffed.

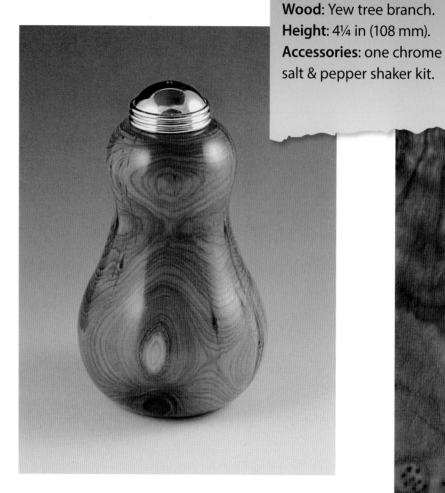

LEVEL OF DIFFICULTY:
BEGINNERS

Wood: Yew tree branch.
Height: 4¼ in (108 mm).
Accessories: one chrome salt & pepper shaker kit.

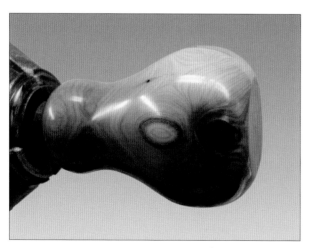

The shaker after having had its base smoothed and finished.

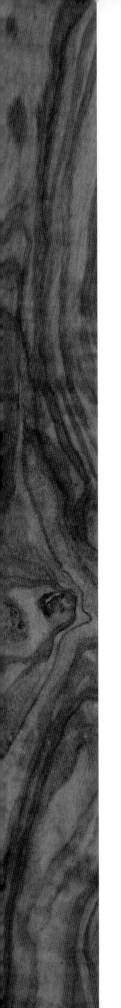

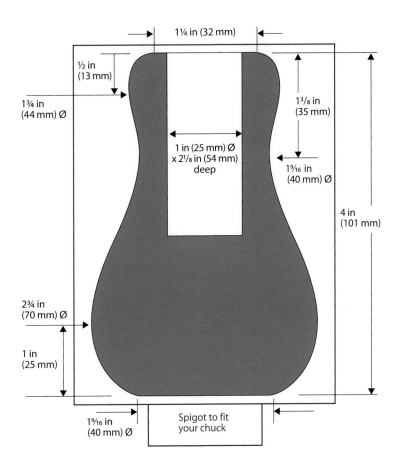

1¼ in (32 mm)

½ in (13 mm)

1¾ in (44 mm) Ø

1 in (25 mm) Ø x 2⅛ in (54 mm) deep

1³⁄₈ in (35 mm)

1⁹⁄₁₆ in (40 mm) Ø

4 in (101 mm)

2¾ in (70 mm) Ø

1 in (25 mm)

1⁹⁄₁₆ in (40 mm) Ø

Spigot to fit your chuck

Drilling and turning the Pear

Blank size: 3 x 3 x 4¾ in (76 x 76 x 120 mm)

Turn the blank with a spigot at what will be the base of the shaker to fit your chuck jaws. Hold by the spigot and face off the top of the pear before drilling and forming the 1 in (25 mm) Ø x 2⅛ in (54 mm) deep hole for the container.

Mark the overall height 4 in (101 mm). Part off at the marked line down to 1⁹⁄₁₆ in (40 mm) Ø. With the tailstock giving support begin shaping the top of the pear.

Next, turn the base. This involves removing the spigot and leaving a nice clean cut.

Remove from the lathe and fit a drive plug as shown in Project 1, the Apple.

Slide the pear over it, ensuring that you have a tight fit and that it is running true. Complete the turning of the pear.

Finally sand, seal and finish.

Because I was using 'cracked' yew I chose to dribble thin superglue (Cyanoacrylate) into the cracks before applying gold gilt cream. After two hours I wiped the excess cream off with a piece of paper towel which had finishing oil on it. Three further coats of finishing oil were applied before buffing.

Make the second shaker, whether it is to be another pear or apple.

The last task is to glue the salt and pepper containers into the shakers. Silicone sealant applied on the sides and at the base of the container will do the job.

3. MODERN

The two halves of the shaker are glued together after the drilling, the turning and the finishing have been completed.

By making these parts separately it actually makes the turning easier. The two separate parts give an interesting and crisp transition between the two halves of the shaker.

The woods used are some I'd never turned before undertaking this project.

They originate from *Mozambique*.

LEVEL OF DIFFICULTY:
BEGINNERS

Wood: Wild mango for the salt, mulumanama for the pepper.
Height: 4½ in (114 mm).
Accessories: two, ¾ in rubber bungs; two small $^{13}\!/_{16}$ in chrome caps.

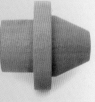

Drive jig held in compression jaws in your chuck

Tailstock end support which uses the live center to support it

$^{13}\!/_{16}$ in chrome cap

Three of the four component parts; the bung is missing from the photo.

Drilling and turning the shaker's body, Part A

Blank size: 3 x 3 x 3½ in
(76 x 76 x 89 mm)

The bung recess hole may need to be a different size depending on the rubber bung you have.
Turn **A**'s blank with a dovetail to fit your chuck jaws.
Hold by the dovetail first and face off the bottom of **A** before drilling and forming the bung recess followed by the ¾ in (19 mm) Ø hole, 2 in (51 mm) deep.
Reverse, holding by the bung recess, measure and mark the overall height 3 in (76 mm). Part off at the marked line removing the dovetail at the same time.
Complete the drilling of the ¾ in (19 mm) hole and form the recess for **B**'s tenon.
Between centers, using the drive plug and tailstock support jig shown, shape the outside of **A**.
Dimensions for the drive plug and tailstock support are shown in *Fig A8-11 & 12* on page 23.
Sand, seal and finish.
Repeat the above for the second shaker.

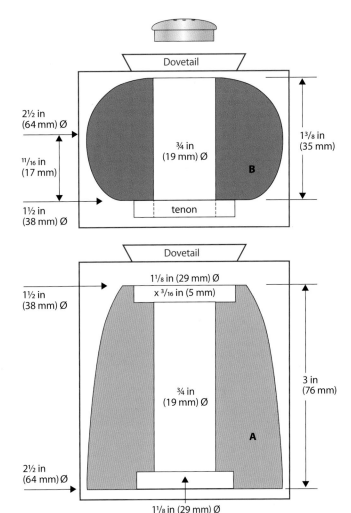

Drilling and turning the shaker's top, Part B

Blank size: 3 x 3 x 2 in
(76 x 76 x 51 mm)

Turn **B**'s blank with a dovetail to fit your chuck jaws.
Hold by the dovetail and face off the bottom before drilling the ¾ in (19 mm) hole through to the dovetail and turning the tenon to fit into **A**.
Reduce the overall diameter to 2½ in (64 mm) Ø. Measure and mark the overall length 1⅜ in (35 mm).

Shape the bottom curve and sand. Begin the turning of the top of the shaker.
Remove from the lathe and hold **B**'s tenon in compression jaws. A live center supports the top of **B** as long as possible. Be sure that everything runs true before shaping **B**.
Alternately, turn a drive plug, ¾ in (19 mm) Ø x 1⅜ in (35 mm) long to support **B** while turning the top of **B**.
Finish turning the top's shape.
Sand, seal and finish the top before gluing **A** to **B**, lining up the grain. Finally, glue in the chrome cap and insert the bung.

4. DUFTON

The shaker is made from two different woods which are first drilled and glued together before shaping.

The fit between the tenons and the recesses should be a good fit, not sloppy, otherwise it makes it difficult to glue.

A & B being glued together.

A being placed on the drive plug which will support the shaker while B is glued in place and its outside turned.

Turning and drilling, Part A

Wood: Acacia
Blank size: 2¾ x 2¾ x 4¼ in
(70 x 70 x 107 mm)

Turn the blank down to a cylinder as shown (red line around drawing).
Hold by the dovetail, supported by a live center in the tailstock. Face off the bottom. Drill or form the bottom bung recess, 1½ in (38 mm) Ø x ³⁄₁₆ in (5 mm) deep.
Drill the 1 in (25 mm) Ø hole, 2 in (51 mm) deep. Sand and seal the base.
Reverse, holding the bung recess hole in expansion jaws with a live center supporting the other end.
Measure, mark and part at the overall length 3½ in (89 mm) removing the dovetail as you go.
Drill a 1 in (25 mm) hole to meet the previously drilled hole before forming the recess for the tenon as shown. Remove from the lathe.
Do NOT turn the outside yet.

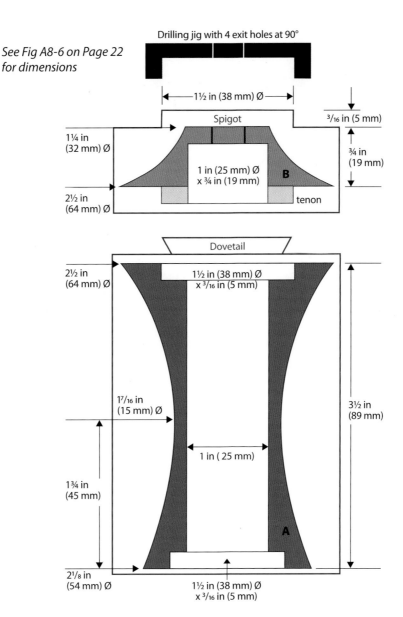

Drilling jig with 4 exit holes at 90°

*See Fig A8-6 on Page 22
for dimensions*

1½ in (38 mm) Ø

³/₁₆ in (5 mm)

Spigot

1¼ in
(32 mm) Ø

¾ in
(19 mm)

1 in (25 mm) Ø
x ¾ in (19 mm)

B

2½ in
(64 mm) Ø

tenon

Dovetail

2½ in
(64 mm) Ø

1½ in (38 mm) Ø
x ³/₁₆ in (5 mm)

1⁷/₁₆ in
(15 mm) Ø

3½ in
(89 mm)

1 in (25 mm)

1¾ in
(45 mm)

A

2¹/₈ in
(54 mm) Ø

1½ in (38 mm) Ø
x ³/₁₆ in (5 mm)

Turning and drilling, Part B

Wood: Walnut
Blank size: 2¾ x 2¾ x 1⁵/₈ in
(70 x 70 x 41 mm)

Turn the blank down to a cylinder, face off and
form the spigot shown. Hold by the spigot and
face off the bottom. Form the 1½ Ø x ³/₁₆ in
tenon to fit into the top of **A**.
Remove from the lathe, reverse, holding by the
tenon and measure, mark the overall length of **B**.
Drill a 1 in (25 mm) hole to a depth of ¾ in
(19 mm). Remove from the lathe and on a drill
press, drill the exit hole(s) as shown using the jig.
Make sure there are no burrs covering the exit
holes in the 1 in (25 mm) hole.

Replace on the lathe by holding the tenon in
compression jaws and shape **B** as shown.
Glue **A** to **B** as shown on page 32.

Shaping the shaker

Turn a drive jig similar to that shown in
Fig A8-10, Page 23, but 3½ in (89 mm) long.
Place it in your chuck.
When running true, the shaker is placed over it
and **A** is shaped.
OR
Hold the base of **A** in expansion jaws.
The potential problem is that there is no support
at the tailstock end. If you can support it then
this is a good way of doing it. Finish as required.

5. MUSHROOM

The mushroom shaker uses a chrome salt cap.

If you don't have one, an alternative is to make a wooden insert of the same diameter with a different kind of wood.

From the drawing you will see that the grain direction for the top of the mushroom is crossways. This has a noticeably visible impact, especially with a light colored wood with a distinctive grain. I used spalted beech.

The shaker should be sanded to 400 grit, finished with a waterproof finish and buffed.

LEVEL OF DIFFICULTY:
BEGINNERS

Wood: Spalted beech.
Height: 4⅜ in (111 mm).
Accessories: two, 1⅜ in chrome caps; two, ¾ in bungs.

Drilling and turning the body, Part A

Blank size: 2¼ x 2¼ x 3½ in
(57 x 57 x 89 mm)

Turn the blank with a dovetail at what will be the top of the shaker's body.
Holding by the dovetail, face off the bottom before forming the ¾ in (19 mm) hole, 3⅛ in deep. Follow this by opening the hole to form the 1¼ in (32 mm) x ³⁄₁₆ in (5 mm) bung recess. Reverse while holding the bung recess in expansion jaws. Mark the overall height 3 in (76 mm).
Part off at the marked line, removing the dovetail as you go.
If the ¾ in (19 mm) hole is not showing, drill through to meet the existing hole.

All of the components.

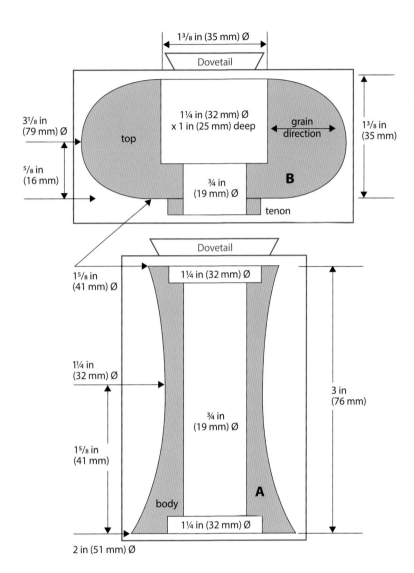

Form a 1¼ in (32 mm) Ø x ³⁄₁₆ in (5 mm) deep recess for B's tenon.

Shape the outside of the body holding it between a wood drive plug as shown in Shaker Jigs *Fig A8-11* on Page 23 and a live center.

Drilling and turning the top, part B

Blank size: 3⅜ x 3⅜ x 2 in
(86 x 86 x 51 mm)

Turn the blank with a dovetail at what will be the top of the shaker. Remove from the lathe and hold the dovetail in compression jaws to face off the bottom of the tenon.

Form the 1¼ in (32 mm) Ø x ³⁄₁₆ in (5 mm) tenon followed by turning the outside diameter to 3⅛ in (79 mm) Ø.

Measure and mark the overall height 1⅜ in (35 mm) and the maximum diameter point at ⅝ in (16 mm) from the bottom.

Drill the ¾ in (19 mm) hole through to the dovetail. Turn the bottom half of **B** and sand. Reverse while holding the tenon in compression jaws and with a live center giving support. Part off at the marked line, removing the dovetail as you go. If necessary, drill a ¾ in (19 mm) hole to meet the existing hole.

Form a 1¼ in (32 mm) Ø x 1 in (25 mm) deep hole for the chrome salt cap to fit into. Finally finish turning the top of B. Sand, seal and finish to your choice. Glue the body and top together on the lathe using the lathe as a clamp before gluing the salt cap in. Finally, glue in the chrome cap and insert the bung.

6. SHAP

I had a problem when it came to giving this shaker a name.

I was given the oak by a family friend who lives in a village called Shap which is in the Lake District National Park in Cumbria, England. It is well known for its bleakness in winter.

I'm not suggesting that this project is bleak!

As you will see the shaker is made of five separate pieces, all of different woods.
However, it is an easy shaker to make. The fit between the tenons and the recesses should be a good fit, not sloppy.

LEVEL OF DIFFICULTY:
BEGINNERS

Wood: Cherry, bubinga, oak, maple and walnut for both shakers.
Height: 3½ in (90 mm).
Accessories: two, ¾ in rubber bungs.

Turning and drilling Part D
Wood: Maple for the salt shaker, walnut for the pepper shaker
Blank size: 1⅛ x 1⅛ x ⅝ in (29 x 29 x 16 mm)

Turn the blank down to a cylinder. Form the dovetail as shown. Hold by the dovetail and face off the bottom.
Form the ¾ in diameter x ³⁄₁₆ in tenon.
Measure a length of ⅜ in (10 mm) and mark.
Reverse while holding **D** by the tenon and face off to the mark.
Draw the template in Fig 1 on paper and glue it onto the top of D and drill the holes.

Drilling Part A
Wood: Bubinga
Blank size: 2³⁄₁₆ x 2³⁄₁₆ x 1⅛ in (56 x 56 x 29 mm)

Turn the blank down to a cylinder.
Form the dovetail as shown.
Hold by the dovetail and face off the bottom.
Drill the ¾ in (19 mm) Ø hole through to the dovetail.
Form a 1⅛ in (29 mm) Ø x ³⁄₁₆ in (5 mm) bung recess.
Measure the overall length ¾ in (19 mm), mark and form the tenon.
Reverse while holding the bung recess hole in expansion jaws.
Part and face off at the marked line, removing the dovetail as you part.

Drilling Part B

Wood: Oak
Blank size: 1⅞ x 1⅞ x 2¾ in
(48 x 48 x 70 mm)

Turn the blank down to a cylinder.
Form the dovetail as shown.
Hold by dovetail and face off the
bottom.
Drill a ¾ in (19 mm) hole approximately
1½ in (38 mm) deep.
Form the 1⅜ in (35 mm) Ø x ³/₁₆ in
(5 mm) in recess to fit the tenon in **A**.
Measure the overall length 2⅜ in
(60 mm) and mark. Reverse while
holding the recess in expansion jaws.
Part and face off at the marked line.
Form the top recess. Drill using a ¾ in
bit through to meet the existing hole.

Drilling Part C

Wood: Cherry
Blank size: 2³/₁₆ x 2³/₁₆ x 1⅛ in
(56 x 56 x 29 mm)

Turn the blank down to a cylinder.
Form the dovetail as shown.
Hold by the dovetail and face off the
bottom.
Form the 1⅜ in (35 mm) Ø x ³/₁₆ in
(5 mm) tenon to fit in **B**'s top recess.
Measure the overall length ⁹/₁₆ in
(14 mm) and mark.
Reverse while holding by the tenon.
Part and face off at the marked line.
Drill the ¾ in hole through.
Form the top recess, 1⅜ in (35 mm) Ø
x ³/₁₆ in (5 mm) .

Turning the shaker

Glue **A**, **B** and **C** together.
Between centers using the jigs shown
on page 30, shape the shaker's body.
Sand, seal and buff the body.
Finish and buff **D** before finally gluing
it into **C**.

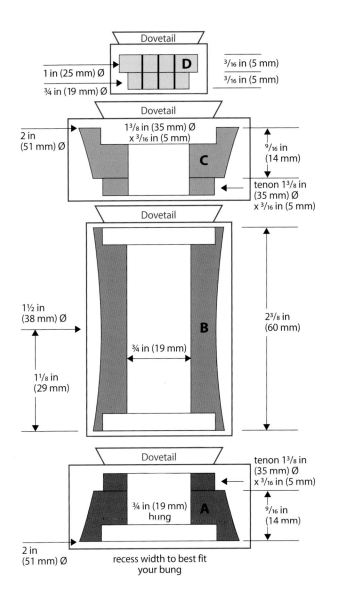

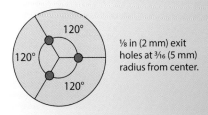

Fig 1. Drilling template

37

7. TAVY

This shaker has three component parts. The top **B**, the base **A** and between them a 'threaded' piece **C**.

For the salt shaker, **A** and **B** are stained blue with a silver gilt cream added. The pepper shaker has been stained red with gold gilt.

C, the thread, will stay as natural olive.

The order of turning is **A**, **B** and then the thread **C** which for page layout purposes is detailed on this page. The shakers are finished with finishing oil.

LEVEL OF DIFFICULTY: BEGINNERS

Wood: Ash and olive.
Height: 2¹³⁄₁₆ in (71 mm).
Accessories: two, ¾ in bungs.

Drilling and turning Component C, *Fig 1*

Wood: Olive
Blank size: 2½ x 2½ x 1¼ in (64 x 64 x 32 mm)

Turn the blank with a dovetail at what will be the top of **C**, to fit your chuck jaws.
Hold by the dovetail to face off the bottom of **C**. Drill the ¾ in (19 mm) hole through to the dovetail. Form the bottom recess.
Reverse while holding by the recess you've just turned, in expansion jaws.
Measure the length ¹⁵⁄₁₆ in (24 mm).

Mark and part at this line, removing the dovetail as you go.
Form the recess for **B**'s tenon.
After turning the outside to 2³⁄₁₆ in (56 mm) Ø, mark the ¼ in (6 mm) lines as shown.
Midway between each of these lines make another line. Using a ½ in skew, form the threads as shown in *Fig 1*. Finally sand, seal and finish.

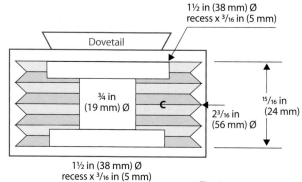

1½ in (38 mm) Ø recess x ³⁄₁₆ in (5 mm)

Dovetail

¼ in (6 mm)
¼ in (6 mm)
¼ in (6 mm)
¼ in (6 mm)

¾ in (19 mm) Ø

C

2³⁄₁₆ in (56 mm) Ø

¹⁵⁄₁₆ in (24 mm)

1½ in (38 mm) Ø recess x ³⁄₁₆ in (5 mm)

Fig 1

Drilling and turning Component A

A Blank size: 2¾ x 2¾ x 1¹³⁄₁₆ in (70 x 70 x 46 mm)

Turn blank **A** with a dovetail at what will be the base of the shaker, to fit your chuck jaws.
Face off and turn the tenon.
Reverse, holding by the tenon.
Drill a ¾ in (19 mm) Ø hole, 1 in (25 mm) deep.
Measure **A**'s length ¾ in (19 mm), mark and part at this line removing the dovetail as you go. Form the recess for the bung hole.
Turn the outside to 2½ in (64 mm) Ø.
Reverse, holding by the recess, shape the outside removing the dovetail as you go. Brush the grain with a brass brush before staining. Ensure that the underside is also covered.
When the stain is dry apply the gilt cream. When dry rub finishing oil over it to remove excess gilt cream.
When dry add further coats of oil.

Drilling and turning Component B

B Blank size: 2¾ x 2¾ x 1⅝ in (70 x 70 x 41 mm)

Turn the exit hole jig as shown.
Mount blank **B** between centers, face off and turn the dovetail. Place the dovetail in chuck jaws. Face off and turn the tenon as in *Fig 2* to fit the jig. Remove from the lathe.
On a drill press, with the jig over the tenon, drill the appropriate exit holes. Remount, holding by the top tenon.
Measure from the tenon 1⅛ in (29 mm) plus the ³⁄₁₆ in (5 mm) bottom tenon to fit in **C**.
Face off and form this tenon.
Drill the ¾ in (19 mm) hole, 1 in (25 mm) deep.
Turn the outside to 2½ in (64 mm) Ø.

top tenon 1½ in (38 mm) Ø x ³⁄₁₆ in (5 mm)

tenon 1½ in (38 mm) Ø x ³⁄₁₆ in (5 mm)

1¹⁄₈ in (29 mm) Ø recess x ³⁄₁₆ in (5 mm)

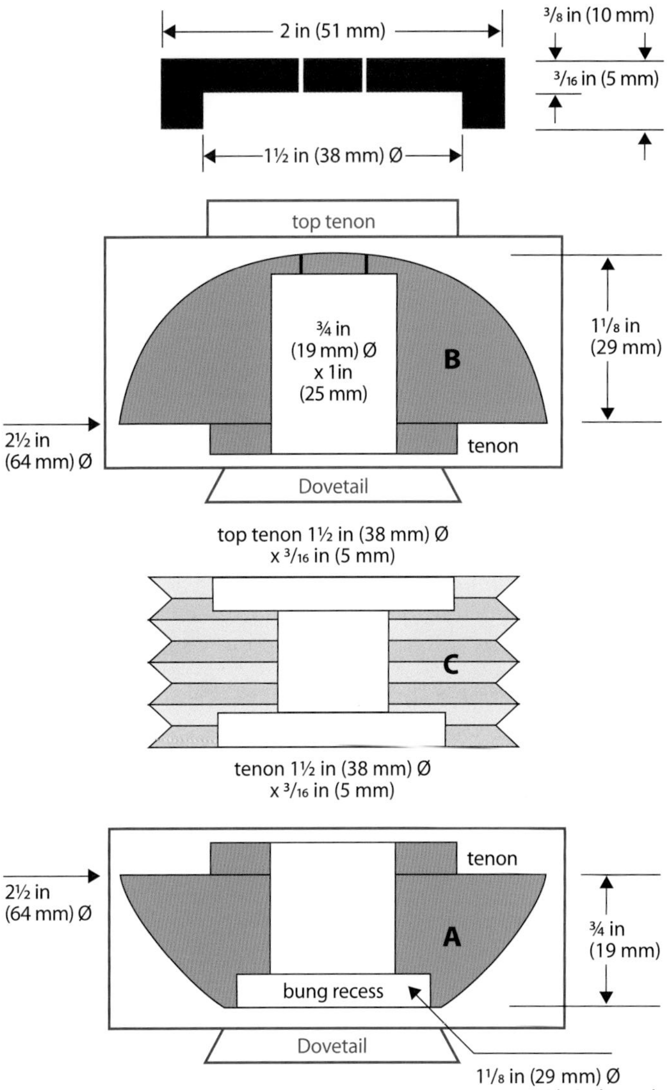

Fig 2

Reverse holding by the bottom tenon and shape, removing the top tenon as you go.
Sand, stain, including the underside of the bottom tenon.
Add gilt cream as part of the finishing process. After further coats of finishing oil the three parts are glued together. Line up the grain as you go.

▶ NOTE: *If you wish, before gluing the three parts they can be lacquered and buffed.*

8. Barrel

As you can see below the shaker is made up of a large number of component parts, eight to be precise.

LEVEL OF DIFFICULTY: EXPERIENCED

Wood: Oak and maple for the salt shaker, oak, maple and bloodwood for the pepper shaker.
Height: 2½ in (64 mm).
Accessories: two, ¾ in rubber bungs.

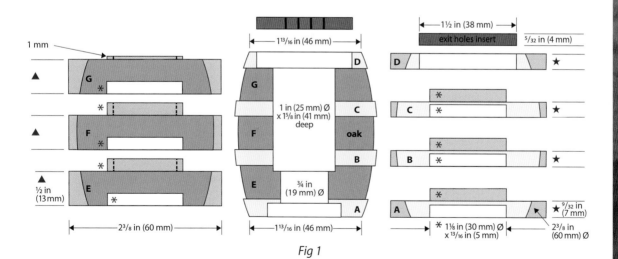

Fig 1

Fig 1 is a busy drawing which shows the way the components **A** through **D** are turned from maple while **E** through **G** are oak.

The seven pieces are turned and fitted together to form the barrel.

Forming Sections A, B, C and D, *Fig 2*

Wood: Maple
Blank size: 2⅝ x 2⅝ x ¾ in
(67 x 67 x 19 mm)

1. Between centers turn the blank down to a bit more than 2⅜ in (60 mm). Face off one end, turn a dovetail.
2. Hold the dovetail in compression jaws. Face off the bottom.
3. Form a recess 1⅛ in (30 mm) x ³⁄₁₆ in (5 mm) as shown.
4. Reverse again, holding the recess in expansion jaws.
5. Measure and mark the overall length, ½ in (13 mm).

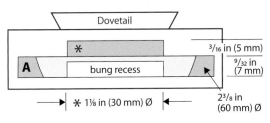

Fig 2

6. Part off, removing the dovetail as you go.
7. Form the tenon as shown.
8. Set aside. Repeat for **B** and **C**.
For **D** follow steps 1 and 2 in *Forming Sections A, B, C and D*.
3. Drill a 1½ in (38 mm) Ø though the blank.
4. Hold the hole in expansion jaws.
5. Measure and mark the overall length ⁹⁄₃₂ in (7 mm) and part off before setting aside.

Forming Sections E, F and G, *Fig 3*

Wood: Oak
Blank size: 2 ⅝ x 2 ⅝ x ¾ in
(67 x 67 x 19 mm)

1. To turn bands **E** and **F**, follow steps 1-4 in *Forming Sections A, B, C and D*.
5. Measure and mark the overall length ¹¹⁄₁₆ in (17 mm) *Fig 3*.
6. Part off, removing the dovetail as you go.
7. Form the tenon as shown. Set aside for now. Repeat for **F**.
For **G**, form a 1¾ in (38 mm) Ø x ⁵⁄₃₂ in (4 mm) tenon for the insert to sit on. See *Fig 1*.
Set aside.
Glue sections **A** through **G** together.

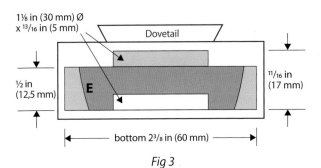

Fig 3

At this stage do not glue the insert in.
The barrel can now be drilled and shaped.
Hold the *insert recess* in expansion jaws.
When running true, drill a ¾ in hole, 1 in (25 mm) deep.
Reverse, holding by the bung recess and drill a hole 1 in (25 mm), 1⅝ in (41 mm) deep.
The barrel can now be held between centers using the drive jig, *Fig A8-11 on Page 23* and a live center to shape the curve as in *Fig 4*.
Sections **E**, **F** & **G**'s diameter should be reduced by approximately ¹⁄₃₂ in (1 mm) only.
Finally turn the exit hole insert as shown in *Fig 1* and drill the number of exit holes you want before gluing it in.
Sand, seal and finish as you choose.

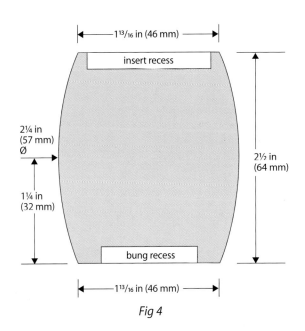

Fig 4

9. CHAMPAGNE CORK

LEVEL OF DIFFICULTY:
INTERMEDIATE

Wood: Ash.
Height: 3⅝ in (92 mm).
Accessories: two, 1 in rubber bungs.

The two halves of the shaker are glued together after the drilling and turning are completed.

By turning the parts separately, it actually makes the turning easier and the separately turned pieces give a crisp transition between the two halves of the shaker.

The shaker should be sanded to 400 grit, finished with a waterproof finish and buffed.

Drilling and turning the shaker's body, Part A

Blank size: 2 x 2 x 2⅜ in
(51 x 51 x 60 mm)

The bung recess hole may need to be a different size depending on the rubber bung you have.

Turn **A**'s blank with a dovetail to fit your chuck jaws.
Hold by the dovetail first and face off the bottom of **A** before drilling and forming the bung recess, (1½ in x 1½ in x ³⁄₁₆ in deep) followed by the ¾ in (19 mm) hole, 2⅛ in (54 mm) deep.
Reverse while holding by the bung recess, measure and mark the overall height 2 in (51 mm). Part off at the marked line, removing the dovetail at the same time.

Drilling the salt hole.

Between centers shape the body by holding the bung recess in expansion jaws and a live center supporting the top of **A**. Otherwise turn a drive plug similar to that shown in *Fig A8-10* on Page 23. Given the size of your live center a tailstock support may also be required.
Sand, seal and finish.
Repeat the above for the second shaker.

Drilling and turning the shaker's top, Part B

B Blank size: 2 x 2 x 2 in
(51 x 51 x 51 mm)

Turn **B**'s blank with a dovetail to fit your chuck jaws.
Hold by the dovetail first and face off the bottom of **B** before turning the tenon and then drilling the ½ in (13 mm) hole, 1⅝ in (41 mm) deep. Measure and mark the overall height 1⅝ in (41 mm).
Shape the bottom and begin turning the top of the shaker.
Reverse, holding by the tenon. For the salt shaker, drill the exit hole on the lathe and for the pepper use the jig in *Fig 1* while the dovetail is still in place.
Shape **B** prior to sanding and finishing as with **A**. Glue **A** and **B** together lining up the grain before clamping on the lathe.

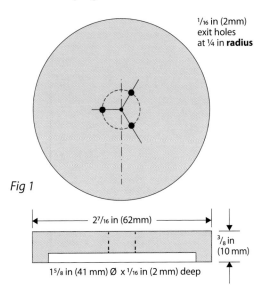

1/16 in (2mm) exit holes at ¼ in **radius**

Fig 1

2⁷/₁₆ in (62mm)

³/₈ in (10 mm)

1⁵/₈ in (41 mm) Ø x ¹/₁₆ in (2 mm) deep

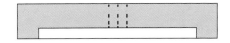

Dovetail to fit the pepper exit holes drilling jig

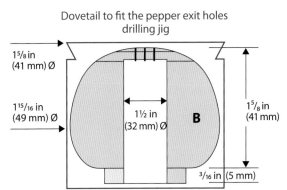

1⁵/₈ in (41 mm) Ø

1¹⁵/₁₆ in (49 mm) Ø

1½ in (32 mm) Ø

B

1⁵/₈ in (41 mm)

³/₁₆ in (5 mm)

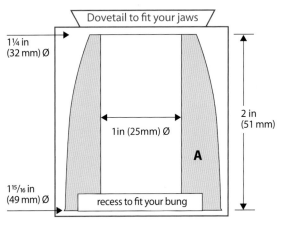

Dovetail to fit your jaws

1¼ in (32 mm) Ø

1in (25mm) Ø

A

2 in (51 mm)

1¹⁵/₁₆ in (49 mm) Ø

recess to fit your bung

Fig 2

After a final sanding and sealing, your chosen finish can be applied.

Drilling and turning the shaker exit holes jig, *Fig 1*

Material: Hardwood, acrylic or corian.
Blank size: 2⅛ x 2⅛ x ½ in
(54 x 54 x 13 mm)

Rough turn, face off the tailstock end before forming a dovetail.
Next, face off the bottom of the jig. Hold by the dovetail and form a recess 2 in (51 mm) x ³/₁₆ in (5 mm) as shown.
Remove from the lathe, reverse and place the recess in expansion jaws. Face off any remaining material near the center point and mark the exit holes as shown. Drill these on a drill press with a ¹/₁₆ in (2 mm) drill.

10. ALCHEMY BOTTLE

LEVEL OF DIFFICULTY: INTERMEDIATE

Wood: Cherry & Masur birch for the salt shaker, walnut & Masur birch for the pepper shaker.
Height: 4⁵⁄₁₆ in (110 mm).
Accessories: two, 1 in rubber bungs.

As you can see below the shaker is made up of three sections. The bottle itself is made up of two parts: the neck and the 'cork', which is turned from Masur birch.

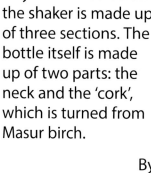
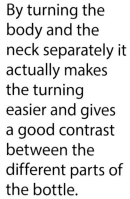

By turning the body and the neck separately it actually makes the turning easier and gives a good contrast between the different parts of the bottle.

Preparing Parts A & B

(A & B) Blank size: 2⅛ x 2⅛ x 5¹⁄₁₆ in (54 x 54 x 130 mm)

First, turn the single blank as shown, adding the **A** and **B** dovetails before parting the two halves.
There will be enough room to create **A**'s dovetail if you have used the correct length blank.

▶ NOTE: Turn **A** first!

Turning and drilling A

Hold **A** by the dovetail and face off the bottom of the bottle.

Drill the bung recess and a 1 in hole, 2½ in (63 mm) deep before turning the outside. Reverse, holding the 1⅜ in hole in expansion jaws or a wooden drive plug. Measure and mark the overall length 3⅛ in (79 mm) before parting off, removing the dovetail as you go. Drill a 1½ in (13 mm) hole to meet the existing hole.

Open up to 11/16 in to allow **B** to fit.

Turn the curve and finish as required.

Turning and drilling B

Hold by the dovetail before facing off and drilling the ⅜ in (10 mm) hole. Shape the outside.

Reverse, holding by the 11⁄16 in (17 mm) tenon. Drill the 11⁄16 in (17 mm) hole in the top as shown. Finish before gluing **A** & **B** together.

Turning and drilling C

Blank size: 1⅝ x 1⅝ x 1⅜ in (41 x 41 x 35 mm)

Follow the procedure as shown for **B** before applying your chosen finish and gluing **C** into (**A** & **B**).

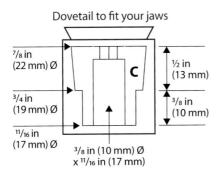

Dovetail to fit your jaws

⅞ in (22 mm) Ø

C

½ in (13 mm)

¾ in (19 mm) Ø

⅜ in (10 mm)

11⁄16 in (17 mm) Ø

⅜ in (10 mm) Ø x 11⁄16 in (17 mm)

The drilling guide is used only for the pepper shaker.

Leave the sides of **C** parallel to allow it to be placed in the guide while drilling takes place. After drilling, remount **C** holding by the 11⁄16 in (17 mm) tenon and slope the top half.

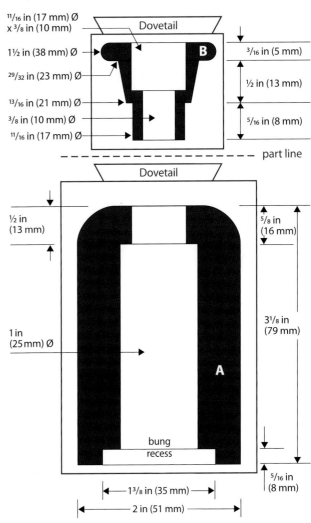

11⁄16 in (17 mm) Ø x ⅜ in (10 mm)

Dovetail

1½ in (38 mm) Ø

29⁄32 in (23 mm) Ø

13⁄16 in (21 mm) Ø

⅜ in (10 mm) Ø

11⁄16 in (17 mm) Ø

B

3⁄16 in (5 mm)

½ in (13 mm)

5⁄16 in (8 mm)

part line

Dovetail

½ in (13 mm)

5⁄8 in (16 mm)

1 in (25 mm) Ø

3⅛ in (79 mm)

A

bung recess

5⁄16 in (8 mm)

1⅜ in (35 mm)

2 in (51 mm)

▶ *NOTE:* The salt exit hole can be drilled using a Jacobs chuck in the tailstock as per *Project 9*.

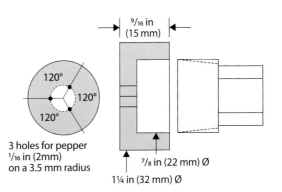

9⁄16 in (15 mm)

120°
120°
120°

3 holes for pepper 1⁄16 in (2mm) on a 3.5 mm radius

⅞ in (22 mm) Ø

1¼ in (32 mm) Ø

11. INK BOTTLE

As you can see the shaker is made up of three sections. The bottle itself is made up of two parts.

The reason the two parts of the bottle are turned separately is to prevent the stain from spreading to the part that represents glass and which must keep its natural wood color.

The caps for both the salt shaker and the pepper shaker are stained black. They are differentiated by the color of the insert and the number of exit holes. Component **A** of one shaker can be stained blue, and for the other shaker, black.

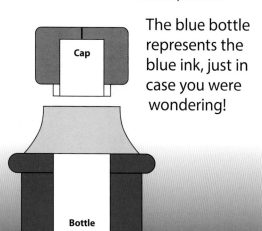

The blue bottle represents the blue ink, just in case you were wondering!

LEVEL OF DIFFICULTY:
INTERMEDIATE

Wood: Maple for both shakers, walnut or a red wood for the insert.
Height: 2⁵⁄₁₆ in (59 mm).
Accessories: two, 1 in rubber bungs.

Turning and drilling Parts A & B
Blank size A: 2¾ x 2¾ x 2 in (70 x 70 x 51 mm)

Rough turn **A** including the dovetail.
Hold by its dovetail, rough turn down to 2⁹⁄₁₆ in (65 mm) and face off the bottom.
Form the 1½ in (38 mm) recess.
Reverse, holding the 1½ in hole in expansion jaws.
Measure and mark the overall length, 1⅝ in (41 mm). Part off at this mark removing the dovetail as you go.
Face off the top.
Form the 1¼ in (32 mm) Ø recess.
Between centers turn the outside as shown.
Stain royal blue or black.

Finally drill the 1 in (25 mm) hole through the center.
Having already stained the outside, the shaker's reservoir will now be clean. Finish as you choose.

Blank size B: 2⅜ x 2⅜ x1⅜ in, (60 x 60 x 35 mm)

Turn as shown with no staining. Glue **A** to **B**.

Turning & drilling the cap, C

Blank size C: 2 x 2 x 1¾ in (51 x 51 x 45 mm)

Rough turn and hold by its dovetail before facing off and drilling a ¾ in (19 mm) hole, 1³⁄₁₆ in (30 mm) deep. Turn the 1 in (25 mm) Ø x ³⁄₁₆ in (5 mm) tenon. Measure the length to ¹⁵⁄₁₆ in (24 mm). Part, removing the dovetail as you go. Reverse, holding by the tenon and supported by a live center. Turn the outside diameter down to 1⁹⁄₁₆ in (40 mm) and round off the bottom corner. Open the ¾ in (19 mm) hole at the top to 1 in (25 mm) diameter to accept the insert.

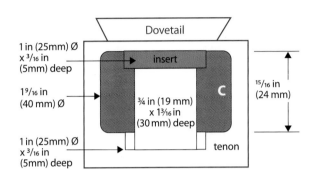

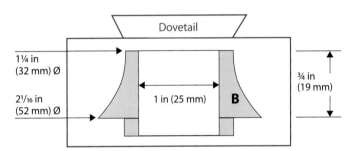

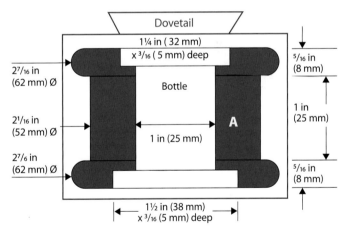

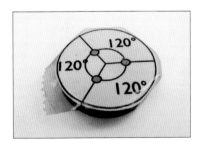

Turning and drilling the insert and its exit holes

Wood: Salt insert is turned from maple and the pepper insert from walnut or a red wood. Turn the insert to fit snugly into the cap. Face off and sand the insert so that it is flush with the cap's top surface. Remove the insert and mark your chosen hole positions on a piece of paper. Stick this on the insert using clear tape as shown.
The exit holes are drilled on a drill press using a ¹⁄₁₆ in (2 mm) twist drill either held directly in a Jacobs chuck or a pin vice chuck.
The cap is stained black and lacquered. Finally seal and finish the insert and glue it into the top of the cap. Align the insert's grain to that of the top of the cap. Finally glue **C** and **B** together.

12. CHIANTI BOTTLE

LEVEL OF DIFFICULTY: INTERMEDIATE

Wood: Ash & Pau Rosa.
Height: 5⅛ in (130 mm).
Accessories: two, ¾ in rubber bungs.

Alternative woods for the top half of the shaker are bloodwood or bubinga.

I was paid the highest compliment achievable when I made a dozen pairs of these shakers for a local Italian restaurant. They were all stolen!

In the photographs of the pair of shakers the inserts at the top are turned from pau amarello (salt shaker) and ebony (pepper shaker). Box or maple are alternatives for the salt insert.

The shakers should be sanded to 400 grit, finished with a waterproof finish and buffed.

The two jigs for drilling the exit holes in the insert at the top of the shaker shown in Fig A8-8 on Page 22.

Insert inside the first jig waiting to be drilled. The kitchen paper (paper towel) removes the slack between the insert and the jig.

Inserts

Turn these after the top has been turned. The size of the two inserts for these shakers is ¹⁹⁄₃₂ in (15 mm) Ø x ⁵⁄₁₆ in (8 mm) thick. As you reduce the diameter keep trying it in **B**, aiming for a snug fit. When completed, put aside.

Drilling and turning base A, *Fig 1*

Blank size: 2½ x 2½ x 2½ in
(64 x 64 x 64 mm)

The bung recess hole may need to be a different size depending on the rubber bung you have.
Turn the blank with a dovetail as shown. Hold by this dovetail and face off the bottom of **A** and drill the bung hole and recess as shown.
Measure and mark the overall height 2 in (51 mm). Turn, sand and seal the bead as shown.
Reverse, holding the bung recess hole in expansion jaws and with a live center in place at the tailstock, before parting at the marked line.
Drill the 1½ in (38 mm) Ø hole. Shape the outside as shown.
Sand and seal the rest of **A**.

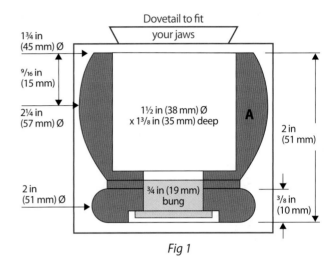

Dovetail to fit your jaws

1¾ in (45 mm) Ø
9/16 in (15 mm)
2¼ in (57 mm) Ø
2 in (51 mm) Ø

1½ in (38 mm) Ø x 1³⁄₈ in (35 mm) deep

A

2 in (51 mm)

¾ in (19 mm) bung

³⁄₈ in (10 mm)

Fig 1

Drilling and turning Part B, *Fig 2*

Blank size: 2 x 2 x 3¾ in
(51 x 51 x 95 mm)

Turn **B**'s blank with a spigot at its top to fit your chuck jaws as shown.
Hold by the spigot first and face off the bottom before drilling the 1¼ in (32 mm) hole, ⁵⁄₈ in (16 mm) deep and the ³⁄₈ in (10 mm) hole, approximately 2½ in (64 mm) deep.
Form the bottom tenon as shown.
Measure and mark the overall height 3⅛ in (79 mm) before parting at this point.
Reverse, holding by the bottom tenon and, when running true, complete the drilling of the ³⁄₈ in (10 mm) Ø reservoir before forming a recess ⁹⁄₁₆ in (14 mm) Ø, ⅛ in (3 mm) deep for the insert.
Supporting the top of **B** with a live center shape, sand and seal.
Turn the inserts and their exit hole(s) using the jigs shown in *Fig A8-8, Page 22*.
Glue the insert into **B**.
The best way I found to shape the top of the insert is by holding **B** by the 1¼ in (32 mm) hole in expansion jaws. Then when running true, very carefully take light cuts with a ³⁄₈ in gouge.
Glue **A** to **B** and when dry, finish and polish.

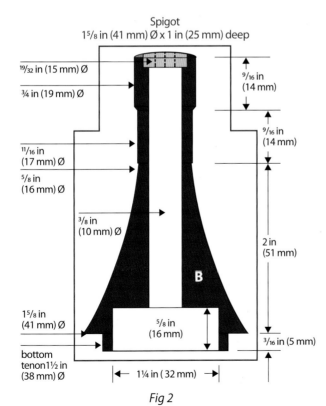

Spigot
1⁵⁄₈ in (41 mm) Ø x 1 in (25 mm) deep

19/32 in (15 mm) Ø
¾ in (19 mm) Ø
9/16 in (14 mm)
9/16 in (14 mm)
11/16 in (17 mm) Ø
⁵⁄₈ in (16 mm) Ø
³⁄₈ in (10 mm) Ø

B

2 in (51 mm)

1⁵⁄₈ in (41 mm) Ø
⁵⁄₈ in (16 mm)
3/16 in (5 mm)

bottom tenon 1½ in (38 mm) Ø

1¼ in (32 mm)

Fig 2

13. FAR EAST CONICAL HAT

LEVEL OF DIFFICULTY:
INTERMEDIATE

Wood: Wild mango for the salt shaker, mulumanama for the pepper shaker.
Height: 3⅝ in (92 mm).
Accessories: two, 1 in rubber bungs.

There are three component parts to this shaker. The body, the top and a hardwood 'false tenon'.

The 'false tenon' makes the shaker's grain appear to run seamlessly between the body and the top. It is turned from any hardwood and glued in to both the top and the body to join them.

As the two parts are turned separately, the junction point between the body and top will demonstrate your turning skills and be much admired.

Preparing a single blank for the shaker, *Fig 2*

Blank size: 3 x 3 x 5 in (76 x 76 x 127 mm)

Rough turn the blank and mark the key measurements.
At the base, turn a spigot to fit your chuck and at the top save wood by turning a similar spigot to fit into compression jaws on your chuck.
At the point where the blank will be split into two, you should have enough wood to easily achieve this. Carefully part at this point.

Turning and drilling the false tenon, *Fig 1*

Blank size: 1⅜ x 1⅜ x 1½ in (35 x 35 x 38 mm)

Wood: Any leftover hardwood you can lay your hands on.
Between centers turn to 1³⁄₁₆ in (30 mm) Ø to fit into the recess in the top of **A** and the bottom of **B**.
Reverse, use a ¾ in (19 mm) drill to form the hole through the tenon. Measure the overall lenght and part at this point.

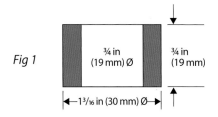

Fig 1

¾ in (19 mm) Ø

¾ in (19 mm)

1³⁄₁₆ in (30 mm) Ø

Turning and drilling the top, B

Hold the top step in compression jaws.
Face off, drill the ¾ in (19 mm) Ø hole to a depth of 1 in (25 mm) and then form the bottom recess for the 'false tenon'.
Turn the outside to the diameter shown and begin forming the bottom curve. Sand the flat area before removing from the lathe. Mark and drill the exit holes on the drill press.
Hold **B** by the step in the top. Glue in the false tenon to the bottom of **B**.
Ensure that the false tenon runs true before gluing it in. Do not glue it into **A** at this time.
When dry, hold the false tenon in compression jaws with a live center giving support for as long as possible.
Shape the outside, sand, seal and finish.

Turning and drilling the base, A

The false tenon should already be glued into **B**.
Hold by the spigot at the bottom and face off the top. Form the recess for the false tenon, trying its fit as you go along.
Do NOT glue in yet.
From this top face, measure and mark back the overall length 2½ in (64 mm) and the 1⁷⁄₁₆ in (37 mm) point.
Part, face off the bottom of the shaker and sand.
Drill 1 in (25 mm) to meet the existing hole.
Form the 1¼ in (32 mm) Ø x ³⁄₁₆ in (5 mm) bung recess.
Between centers, shape the outside, sand, seal, finish and put aside.
Glue **A** and **B** together.

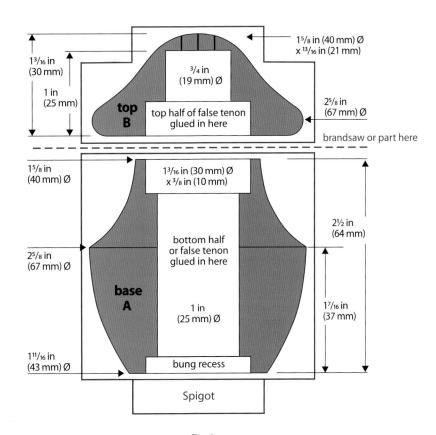

Fig 2

14. BEEHIVE

As you can see from the photograph and *Fig 1*, each sections is turned from a different type of wood.

One big advantage of this is the ease of turning and the crispness it brings to the shaker. The small price to pay is in time taken turning each of the sections.

The height of the shaker, 2⅝ in (67 mm), determined the thickness of sections **A** through I which are 7.5 mm each.

Both shakers have an Identification

LEVEL OF DIFFICULTY: INTERMEDIATE

Wood: See table for the types of wood used and blank sizes.
Height: 2⅝ in (67 mm).
Accessories: two, ¾ in rubber bungs.

(ID) insert to better indicate the contents. Your bung may be a different size and require different size holes for it and the reservoir.

▶ NOTE: As you will notice in *Fig 1*, the colors of the wood go from dark **A** through to near white **I**.
This is intentional as it gives a more pleasing esthetic look to the shakers.
The tenons are: 1½ x 1½ x ³⁄₁₆ in (38 x 38 x 5 mm).
Make the sections up as pairs for both shakers as you go along.

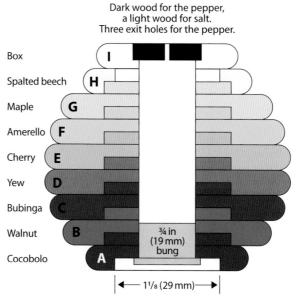

Dark wood for the pepper, a light wood for salt. Three exit holes for the pepper.

Box   **I**

Spalted beech   **H**

Maple   **G**

Amerello   **F**

Cherry   **E**

Yew   **D**

Bubinga   **C**

Walnut   **B**   ¾ in (19 mm) bung

Cocobolo   **A**

◄— 1⅛ (29 mm) —►

Fig 1

Section A, *Fig 2*

Blank size: 2 x 2 x ⅝ in (51 x 51 x 16 mm)

Turn the blank as shown. Hold by the dovetail and face off the bottom before measuring the 7.5 mm width and forming the bead using the tool of your choice (a skew or a spindle gouge for example).
Next, drill the two holes shown in *Fig 2*.
The size you choose will depend on your bung size. Reverse, hold the bung recess to form the 1½ in (38 mm) Ø x ³⁄₁₆ in (5 mm) deep tenon.

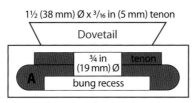

1½ (38 mm) Ø x ³⁄₁₆ in (5 mm) tenon
Dovetail
¾ in (19 mm) Ø | tenon
A
bung recess
1⅛ (29 mm) Ø x ³⁄₁₆ in (5 mm)

Fig 2

After sanding, finish as you please. I chose to use cellulose sealer and melamine lacquer before buffing with tripoli, white diamond and wax. Gluing is held back until all of the sections have been completed.

Sections B through G

These blanks all need to be a minimum of ⅝ in (16 mm) thick. Turn the blank to have an outside diameter 2 mm larger than shown in *Fig 4*.
Face off one side and form a dovetail to fit your chuck jaws.
Hold by the dovetail, face off the opposite face and form a 1½ in (38 mm) Ø x 5 mm recess to fit snugly in the next bead's tenon.

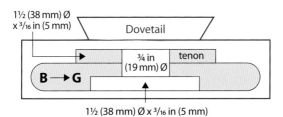

1½ (38 mm) Ø
x ³⁄₁₆ in (5 mm)
Dovetail
¾ in (19 mm) Ø | tenon
B → G
1½ (38 mm) Ø x ³⁄₁₆ in (5 mm)

Fig 3

SECTION	DIAMETER Ø mm	WIDH mm	WOOD USED
A	48	7.5	Cocobolo
B	64	7.5	Walnut
C	70	7.5	Bubinga
D	74	7.5	Yew
E	74	7.5	Cherry
F	70	7.5	Amerello/Yellowheart
G	64	7.5	Maple
H	52	7.5	Spalted beech
I	42	7.5	Box
Insert	25	5	Amerello
Insert	25	5	Ebony

Fig 4

Measure 7.5 mm for the bead's width and turn using either a ½ in skew, or a detail gouge.
Drill a ¾ in (19 mm) Ø hole through the blank.
Reverse, holding the recess in expansion jaws, form a 1½ in (38 mm) Ø x 5 mm tenon.
Sand and seal.

Sections H and I, *Fig 5*

H is the same as **B** through **G** except that there are two recesses; one, 1½ in (38 mm) Ø x ³⁄₁₆ in (5 mm) and the other, 1³⁄₁₆ in (30 mm) Ø x 4 mm. See *Fig 1*.
I is a little different. The 1³⁄₁₆ in (30 mm) Ø tenon is formed while being held by the dovetail followed by the 7.5 mm bead.
The ¾ in (19 mm) hole is drilled through before the section is reversed and the dovetail removed. The ⅞ in (22 mm) Ø recess for the insert ID is formed. Once the insert has been glued in and it is dry, face off, sand and finish.

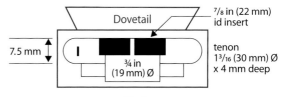

Dovetail
⅞ in (22 mm) id insert
7.5 mm
I
tenon 1³⁄₁₆ in (30 mm) Ø x 4 mm deep
¾ in (19 mm) Ø

Fig 5

For help with the turning and drilling of the ID insert, see the last section of *Project 11, The Ink Bottle shaker: Turning and drilling the cap C.*
The final task is to glue the sections together and be careful to ensure that the glue does not squeeze out between the sections.
Ensure that the grain of each section is in the same direction.
The end result should be a lovely pair of shakers to grace your dining table…

15. OUSBY

This project takes the longest to turn, with 17 inlay holes to drill and the same number of inlays to turn. It is probably the most satisfying when you have finished it.

The shaker has four columns of different sized circular inlays in it. The columns are drilled along the center line of the four sides of the rectangular blank. The holes are best drilled on a drill press. Try to ensure that all of the inlays grain direction line up with the wood it is being glued into.

Turning and drilling the top, *Fig 1*

Blank: 2 x 2 x ¾ in (51 x 51 x 19 mm)

Start by turning the ¾ in (19 mm) Ø inlays No's 1- 4 ¾ in (19 mm) long, using the types of wood shown in *Fig 1*. Mark out the 2 x 2 x ¾ in square blanks as in *Fig 1*. The 4 outer inlays will be at 90° to each other with their centers on a ¹¹/₃₂ in (9 mm) radius. Begin the drilling with 1 then glue in the inlay 1. Drill 2 and glue in 2 etc.
Turn 5 *Fig 1*, parting it at 23 mm to allow a live center to be placed on it.
Drill 5's exit holes at this point in time.
Between centers face off and form the dovetail as shown in *Fig 3*.
Hold by the dovetail and turn the outside to 1¾ in (45 mm) Ø, before measuring and marking

the overall length and the tenon, ⁹/₁₆ in (15 mm). Face off and turn the tenon. Drill the 1 in (25 mm) hole, ⅜ in (10 mm) deep.
Reverse, holding by the tenon to face off the top, removing the dovetail as you go to give a height of 10 mm, *Fig 3*. Sand and seal.

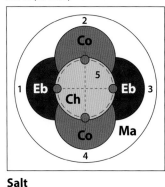

All inlays are ¾ in (19 mm) Ø x ¾ in (19 mm)

Salt

exit holes not shown — ¹¹/₃₂ in (9 mm) radius

Pepper

⅞ in (22 mm) outer radius

● = center for drilling
Ch = Cherry; Co = Cocobolo; Ma = Maple; Eb = Ebony; Wa = Walnut

Fig 1

Drilling and turning the body, *Fig 2*

Blank: 2 x 2 x 3¾ in (51 x 51 x 95 mm)

Fig 2 below shows the four sides of the body and the key dimensions. Mark out and drill the holes approximately ½ in deep on a drill press. If you have other attractive woods to use, then do so. Glue each inlay in as you go, lining up the grain with the side's grain. When completed, between centers turn the blank down to 1⅞ in (48 mm) Ø and turn the dovetail as in *Fig 3*. Holding by the dovetail, face off the bottom and drill the 1 in (25 mm) hole 2 in (51 mm) deep. Use a ½ in skew to open the bung recess to 1¼ in (32 mm) Ø x 3/16 in (5 mm).

Turning the outside of the shaker's body, *Fig 3*

Reverse, holding the bung recess in expansion jaws, measure the overall length, mark and part off, removing the dovetail as you go.
Glue the body to its top before turning down to 1¾ in (44 mm) Ø. Sand, seal and finish. It would be nice if the bung recess could safely support the shaker by itself while being turned. A live center in the tailstock cannot be brought up to support the shaker without marking the top, so use a drive plug with a length of 2¾ in (70 mm) to hold the shaker in place while the outside is turned down to a diameter of 1¾ in (44 mm). If the drive plug is not tight enough in the shaker, wrap masking tape around it to give a tight fit. Sand, seal and finish as you prefer.

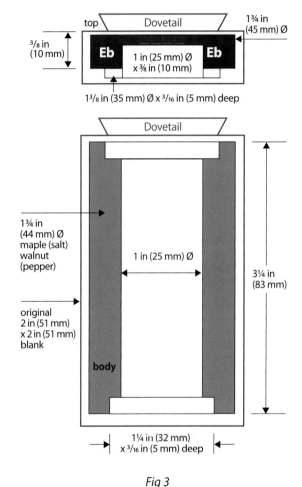

top   Dovetail   1¾ in (45 mm) Ø

3/8 in (10 mm)

Eb   1 in (25 mm) Ø x 3/8 in (10 mm)   Eb

1⅜ in (35 mm) Ø x 3/16 in (5 mm) deep

Dovetail

1¾ in (44 mm) Ø maple (salt) walnut (pepper)

1 in (25 mm) Ø

3¼ in (83 mm)

original 2 in (51 mm) x 2 in (51 mm) blank

body

1¼ in (32 mm) x 3/16 in (5 mm) deep

Fig 3

Inlays
A3, B1, C3, D1 = ½ in (13 mm) Ø - Cherry
A2, B2, C2, D2 = ¾ in (19 mm) Ø - Cocobolo
A1, B3, C1, D3 = 1 in (25 mm) Ø - Ebony

Body wood:
Walnut (pepper) and Maple (salt)

Fig 2

D
D1
¾ in (19 mm)
D2
1 in (25 mm)
D3
7/8 in (22 mm)

mark this, face off line

A
A1
A2
A3
bottom

B
B1
B2
B3

C
C1
1 in (25 mm)
C2
¾ in (19 mm)
C3
5/8 in (16 mm)

55

16. STONEWARE JAR SPICE SHAKER

LEVEL OF DIFFICULTY:
INTERMEDIATE

Wood: Spalted beech, walnut, Masur birch and cherry.
Height: 3¾ in (95 mm).
Accessories: one, 1 in (25 mm) bung; 1 silicone sealing ring.

This is the first shaker project which is designed to be used for spices other than salt and pepper.

There are four components in this shaker.

The body **A**, the top **B**, a cork **C** and an insert for the exit holes.

Three different woods are used to give it some degree of authenticity.

Component parts.

1¼ in (32 mm) Ø

9/16 in (14 mm) Ø

*The insert shown is glued into **B**.*

Shaker's cork with its silicone sealing ring on.

Drilling and turning the insert

Blank size: 1½ x 1½ x 1 in (38 x 38 x 25 mm)
Wood: cherry

Turn a round piece of cherry, 1¼ in (32 mm) Ø x ³⁄₁₆ in (5 mm) thick.
My recommendation is that you drill five holes as shown, ¹⁄₁₆ in (2 mm) Ø.
This size hole is suitable for any spice that has a 'flour-like' consistency. For spices such as seeds or flakes increase the diameter of the holes.

Drilling and turning A

Blank size: 2¼ x 2¼ x 2⅝ in
(57 x 57 x 66 mm)
Wood: Spalted beech

Rough turn the blank with a dovetail on the top.
Hold by the dovetail and face off the bottom before drilling a 1 in (25 mm) Ø x 1¼ in (32 mm) deep hole for the bung.
Open up a recess ³⁄₁₆ in (5 mm) deep suitable for your bung.
Reverse, holding the recess in expansion jaws. When running true, measure and mark the overall height 2⅜ in (60 mm).
Part off at the marked line removing the dovetail as you go.
Drill a 1¼ in (32 mm) hole, 1¼ in (32 mm) deep. Form a recess, 1½ in (38 mm) Ø by ³⁄₁₆ in (5 mm) deep.
Turn the outside diameter to 2 in (51 mm) Ø.
Sand, seal and finish as you choose.

Drilling and turning B

Blank size: 2¼ x 2¼ x 1¼ in
(57 x 57 x 32 mm)
Wood: Walnut

Rough turn between centers and turn a dovetail at the top.
Hold by the dovetail, face off the bottom before turning a tenon to fit into the top of **A**.
Drill a 1¼ in (32 mm) Ø hole, ⁵⁄₁₆ in (8 mm) deep. Follow this with a 1 in (25 mm) Ø hole, ¾ in (19 mm) deep.
This hole will probably pass through the dovetail. Reverse, holding the tenon in compression jaws.
Measure ¹³⁄₁₆ in (21 mm), mark and part at this line with the live center in place.
Turn the bead to the dimensions shown.
Reverse, holding by the 1 in (25 mm) Ø to finish shaping the outside.
Sand, seal and finish as with **A**.

Fig 1

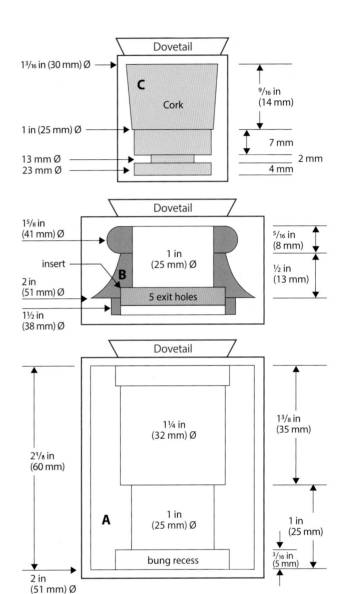

Drilling and turning C

Blank size: 1¼ x 1¼ x 1⅝ in
(32 x 32 x 41 mm)
Wood: Masur birch

Between centers, rough turn and add a dovetail to the top. Holding by the dovetail face off the bottom of **C**. Shape as shown. Use a very fine parting tool to form a ¹⁄₁₆ in (2 mm) wide slot for the silicone sealing ring, shown in *Fig 1*.
An old, large hacksaw blade which has had its teeth ground away and the handle sheathed for safety, works.
Sand, seal and finish the cork as with **A**. The gluing order is: the insert into **B** and then **B** into **A**.

17. EL PASO SPICE SHAKER

It is recommended that you read through the instructions before starting. This spice shaker incorporates an air-tight top plug, with a silicone sealing ring.

The spice is contained in a clear acrylic tube, **E**. The shaker is made up of several different components. While the pieces are not too difficult to turn, they do need accurate measurement and turning.

The number and size of holes in the insert is your choice to meet your spice needs.

**LEVEL OF DIFFICULTY:
EXPERIENCED**

Wood: Purple heart, maple and holly.
Height: 3¹⁵⁄₁₆ in (100 mm).
Accessories: one, 1 in rubber bung; one silicone sealing ring; one clear acrylic tube, 32 mm OD. (See *Suppliers* section for sources).

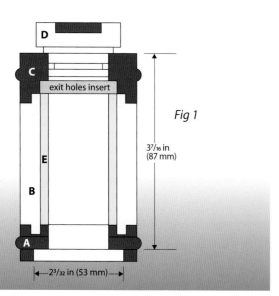

Fig 1

3⁷⁄₁₆ in (87 mm)

2³⁄₃₂ in (53 mm)

exit holes insert

Drilling and turning the top plug, D

Blank size: 1¾ x 1¾ x 1⅞ in
(44 x 44 x 48 mm)
Wood: Holly and purple heart inlay.

After rough turning hold by the dovetail to face off and mark out the key lengths. Begin forming the 2 mm slot for the silicone sealing ring. Glue the insert and shape the plug. Sand, seal and finish.

due to the accuracy required all dimentions are metric

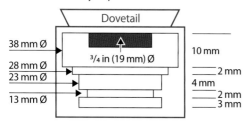

Dovetail

38 mm Ø
28 mm Ø
23 mm Ø
13 mm Ø

¾ in (19 mm) Ø

10 mm
2 mm
4 mm
2 mm
3 mm

All of the components.

Drilling and turning the base, A

Blank size: 2¼ x 2¼ x ⅞ in
(57 x 57 x 22 mm)
Wood: Purple heart

Hold by the dovetail, face off and drill/form the holes for the bung recess. Reverse, measure, mark and part the overall length before forming the bead and the recess to receive **B**.

Drilling and turning the body, B

Blank size: 2¼ x 2¼ x 2⅞ in
(57 x 57 x 73 mm)
Wood: Maple

The blank has a 1 in (25 mm) Ø hole drilled in the face of each side at a different position.
Mark each face and drill to a depth of ¾ in (19 mm). Mount between centers, rough turn and form the dovetail. Hold by the dovetail to face off and form the 1⅝ in (41 mm) step for joining to **A**. Drill a 1¼ in (32 mm) Ø hole, 1½ in (38 mm) deep. Carefully open up this hole to loosely receive the tube.
Reverse and, when running true measure, and part at the marked length before drilling the hole to meet the existing hole and forming the step for joining to **C**.

Drilling and turning C

Blank size: 2¼ x 2¼ x 1¼ in
(57 x 57 x 32 mm)
Wood: Purple heart

Hold by the dovetail, drill/form a 1⅝ in (41 mm) Ø x 3/16 in (5 mm) recess. Drill a 1 in (25 mm) hole through to the dovetail. Open up a recess for the insert 1¼ in (32 mm) x 4 mm deep.
Reverse, holding by the 1⅝ in (41 mm) Ø recess. Measure, mark and part off the length to ⅞ in (22 mm).

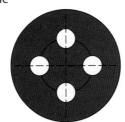

1¼ in (32 mm) Ø x 3/16 in (5 mm)

exit holes insert

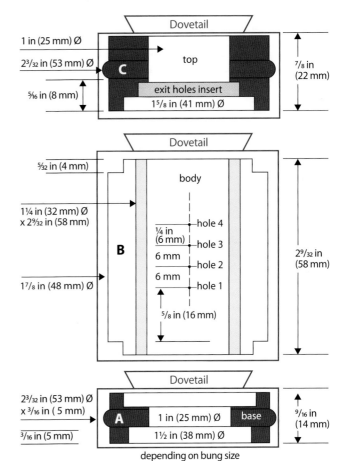

Dovetail

top

1 in (25 mm) Ø

2³/32 in (53 mm) Ø

C

exit holes insert

5/16 in (8 mm)

1⅝ in (41 mm) Ø

⅞ in (22 mm)

Dovetail

body

5/32 in (4 mm)

1¼ in (32 mm) Ø x 2 9/32 in (58 mm)

B

¼ in (6 mm) — hole 4

— hole 3

6 mm

— hole 2

6 mm

1⅞ in (48 mm) Ø

— hole 1

5/8 in (16 mm)

2 9/32 in (58 mm)

Dovetail

2³/32 in (53 mm) Ø x 3/16 in (5 mm)

A

1 in (25 mm) Ø

base

3/16 in (5 mm)

1½ in (38 mm) Ø

9/16 in (14 mm)

depending on bung size

Drilling and turning the exit hole insert

Blank size: 1½ x 1½ x 1in (38 x 38 x 25 mm)
Wood: Purple heart

Turn the blank to a cylinder and reduce to be a snug fit in **C**. Place masking tape over the face of the insert to allow you to place pencilled centers to help position the location of the holes you have chosen. Part off to 5 mm thickness. Drill, sand and seal.

Turning the outside of the shaker

Glue **A** to **B**. Glue the base of the acrylic tube to **A**. Glue the insert to **C**. Glue **C** to (**A** & **B**). Turn the outside including its beads as shown. Sand, seal and finish.

18. SANTA FÉ SPICE SHAKER

This is the last shaker project. It is dedicated to my wife who loves to have cinnamon on her cappuccino coffee. I know on which side my bread is buttered!

There are four turned components in this shaker. The body **A**, an insert for the exit holes **C**, a sleeve **D** and the top **E**.

You may want to consider a separate tenon in the top lid **F**. Reason? If you turn the 23 mm Ø too small it will be a loose fit and no longer airtight.

LEVEL OF DIFFICULTY:
INTERMEDIATE

Wood: Bubinga.
Height: 3⅜ in (85 mm).
Accessories: one, 1 in (25 mm) bung; one silicone sealing ring; one clear acrylic tube 1¼ in (32 mm) OS, 1¹⁄₃₂ in (26 mm) ID.

Drilling and turning A

Blank size: 2¼ x 2¼ x 2⅝ in (57 x 57 x 67 mm)
Wood: Bubinga

Rough turn the blank with a spigot on the top. Hold by the spigot and face off the bottom of **A**, before drilling or forming a 1⅜ in (35 mm) Ø x ³⁄₁₆ in (5 mm) deep hole for the bung's recess. Follow this with a 1 in (25 mm) hole for a depth of ⅜ in (10 mm).
Reverse, holding the recess in expansion jaws. When running true, measure and mark the overall height 2¼ in (57 mm).
Part off at the marked line removing the spigot as you go.

The insert is shown glued into A.

Drill a 1¼ in (32 mm) hole, 1¾ in (44 mm) deep for the acrylic tube.
Turn the outside diameter to 2³⁄₁₆ in (56 mm).
Mark the position of the two ⁵⁄₁₆ in (8 mm) beads. Turn the beads using the tool you prefer: beading tool, skew or detail gouge. Sand and seal before putting aside.

Component parts.

Preparing B

Cut a length of clear acrylic tube, see accessories on p. 60 for size of the tube. The length should be 26 mm.

Drilling and turning the insert, C

Blank size: 1½ x 1½ x 1 in
(38 x 38 x 25 mm)

Turn a round piece of bubinga, 1¼ in (32 mm) Ø x ³⁄₁₆ in (5 mm) thick.
My recommendation is that you drill the four holes, ³⁄₁₆ in (5 mm) Ø.
This size hole is suitable for any spice that has a 'flour-like' consistency, like cinnamon. For other types of spice increase the diameter of the holes.

Fig 1

1¼ in (32 mm) Ø

½ in (13 mm) Ø

Drilling and turning D

Turn the wood of your choice 1¼ in (32 mm) Ø x ½ in (13 mm) long, with a 1 in (25 mm) hole through it.

Drilling and turning E

Blank size: 2¼ x 2¼ x 1¼ in
(57 x 57 x 32 mm)

Rough turn between centers and turn a dovetail at the top. Hold by the dovetail, face off the bottom before turning a 23 mm Ø tenon. Add the 2 mm slot for the silicone sealing ring.
Turn the outside down to 2³⁄₁₆ in (56 mm) Ø. Form the bead, measure and mark the ½ in (13 mm) line and start turning the top curve. Reverse, holding the tenon in expansion jaws.
Taking your time, finish turning the top curve and finial. Keep the live center in place as long as possible to give support. Sand and seal. Set aside.
If you choose to turn a separate 'false tenon' then follow the next procedure. If not ignore.

Drilling and turning the false tenon, F

Blank size: 1¼ x 1¼ x 1⅝ in
(32 x 32 x 41 mm)

Between centers, rough turn and turn a dovetail on the top. Holding by the dovetail, face off the bottom of **F**. Shape as shown. Use a very fine parting tool to form the 2 mm slot for the silicone sealing ring.
Sand, seal and glue into the drilled hole in **E**. Finish the top.
The assembly and gluing order is: place silicone sealing ring over the top's tenon **F** and into the 2 mm slot.
Glue tube **B**, using silicone sealer, into **A**; insert **C** is glued to **A**; **D** is glued to **C**.

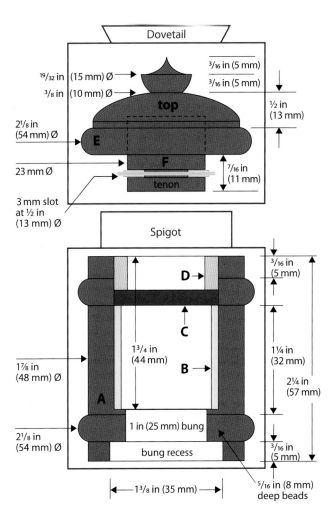

Fig 2

19. MORTAR AND PESTLE

LEVEL OF DIFFICULTY:
INTERMEDIATE

Wood: Maple.
Height: 4 in (101 mm).

All credit for this project goes to Ian Woodford.

It is his design; one which I admire very much and feel I could not improve on. So with his permission, here it is.

Fig 1

⅞ in (22 mm) radius

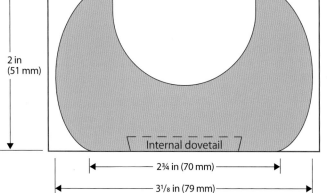

1¾ in (44 mm)

Recess A

2 in (51 mm)

1³⁄₁₆ in (30 mm)

Internal dovetail

2¾ in (70 mm)

3⅛ in (79 mm)

Fig 2

Turning the Mortar

Blank size: 3¼ x 3¼ x 2¼ in (83 x 83 x 57 mm)

Templates can be made from thick cardboard or thin pieces of wood.
Begin by drilling **Recess A** on a drill press, see *Fig 2*. Mount the blank by holding the **Recess A** in expansion jaws.
Clean up the base of the mortar turning it slightly concave. Form an internal dovetail in the base as shown.

Sand the base to 400 grit. Begin turning the outside base curve using a spindle gouge.
Reverse the blank, gripping the base recess in expansion jaws.
Begin the hollowing out of the mortar to get the shape. Throughout the hollowing the template, *Fig 1*, is used. To finish the inside shaping I used a ½ in round scraper until the shape was as shown. Finally the rest of the mortar is sanded. No finish was applied although a food safe finish can be used.

Finished pestel with no finish applied. Hard, tight grained non toxic woods are best. Maple is ideal.

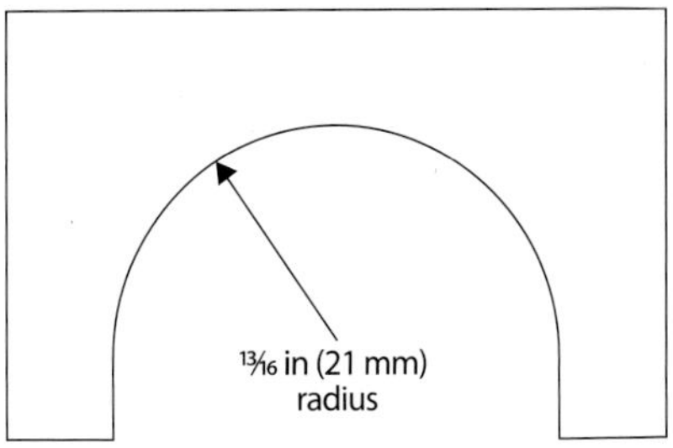

Fig 3

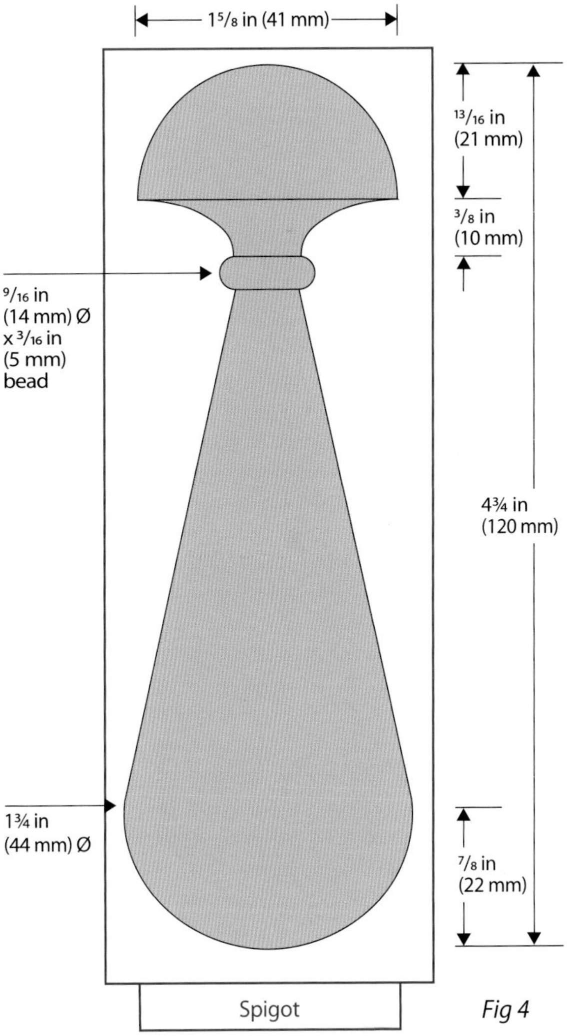

$^{13}/_{16}$ in (21 mm) radius

$1^5/_8$ in (41 mm)

$^{13}/_{16}$ in (21 mm)

$^3/_8$ in (10 mm)

$^9/_{16}$ in (14 mm) Ø x $^3/_{16}$ in (5 mm) bead

$4^3/_4$ in (120 mm)

$1^3/_4$ in (44 mm) Ø

$^7/_8$ in (22 mm)

Spigot

Fig 4

$^7/_8$ in (22 mm) radius

Fig 5

Turning the Pestle, *Fig 4*

Blank size: 2 x 2 x 5¾ in
(51 x 51 x 147 mm)

The blank, *Fig 4*, is mounted between centers, rough turned and a spigot added to fit your compression jaws.

Hold the spigot in your chuck and initially bring the tailstock up for support. Turn the handle's top dome using a ⅜ in gouge and the Template, *Fig 3*, to check as you go.

Measure and mark the key dimensions before shaping the underside of the handle being careful not to reduce the diameter required for the bead.

The bead can be formed using a variety of tools like a ½ in skew or a ¼ in detail gouge.

I used a 5 mm fluted parting tool.

The central part is shaped using a ½ in skew. For the dome at the base of the pestle use a ⅜ in spindle gouge. Begin turning the dome, checking with the template shown in *Fig 5* as you go along.

The two ends can be cleaned up and sanded off the lathe.

The mortar's internal holding recess.

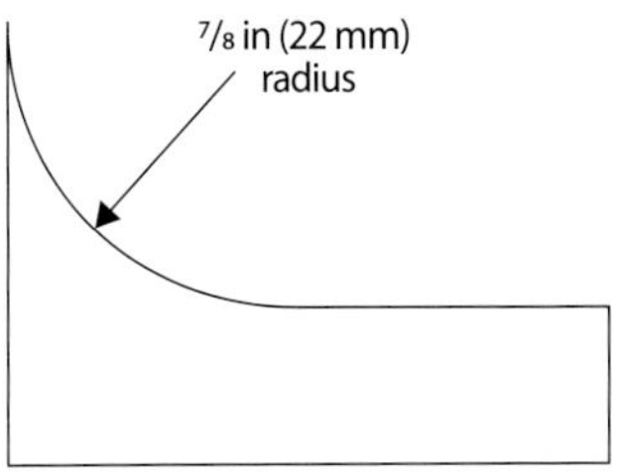

20. SHAKER STAND

LEVEL OF DIFFICULTY:
BEGINNERS

Wood: Various.
Size: 3½ in (89 mm) Ø
x ½ in (13 mm).

My original idea was to design a shaker stand onto which a pair of shakers could be placed.

What actually evolved during the design phase were stacking shaker/wine coasters!

So, with this last project, you are getting two for the price of one. Before you get started cutting up the blanks, note the grain direction, cross grain.

They are very easy to turn. The key thing is the finish you apply to them.

Scraps of wood from other projects could be used.

When used as coasters they invariably get wet and/or have heat applied to them, so...

The shakers are finished with several coats of a waterproofing wood finish like melamine lacquer. Alternatively, cork liners could be used.

A stack of six stands or, in this case, coasters. All made from different woods.

A shaker stand with the Modern shaker sitting on it.

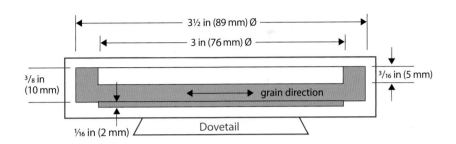

Dimensions shown in diagram:
- 3½ in (89 mm) Ø
- 3 in (76 mm) Ø
- ³/₈ in (10 mm)
- ³/₁₆ in (5 mm)
- grain direction
- ¹/₁₆ in (2 mm)
- Dovetail

Turning a shaker stand/coaster

Blank size: 4 x 4 x 1 in
(101 x 101 x 25 mm)

Rough turn the blank with a dovetail at what will be the bottom of the stand, to fit your chuck jaws. Hold by the dovetail to face off the top. Form the recess, ³/₁₆ in (5 mm) deep.
Turn the outside of the stand to a diameter of 3½ in (89 mm). Sand.

Reverse, holding the recess in expansion jaws or on a wooden jam chuck.
Measure and mark the height of the stand, 12 mm. Part just above this point, removing the dovetail as you go.
Form a 2 mm tenon as shown which will be able to sit in the top of the stand below it.
Clean up the base of the stand and sand it and apply a waterproof finish.

A group of shakers and stands.

SUPPLIERS

This list is not exhaustive; there may be other excellent suppliers that I am unaware of.

UK
Axminster Power Tool Centre Ltd
www.axminster.co.uk
Tel. 0800 371822
Synthetic finishing pads, Silicone sealing rings

Chestnut Products
www.chestnutproducts.co.uk
Tel. 01473 425878
Chestnut colour stains, sanding sealers and lacquer finishes

Turners Retreat
www.turners-retreat.co.uk
01302 744344
1 in rubber bung. Code: PRB
Salt & pepper shaker containers.
Code: CSPK

Chasingbutterfliesboutique
Ebay seller
www.ebay.co.uk
Search word string : *Salt & pepper pot bung*
¾ in & 1 in rubber bungs
Mobile: 07917114441

Clear Plastic Supplies
http://clearplastictube.co.uk
01246 270992
(1¼ in) 32 mm x 3 mm x 500 mm
Clear Acrylic Tube (Extruded)

USA AND CANADA
Craft Supplies USA
www.woodturnerscatalog.com
Tel. 1-800-551-8876
¾ in salt shaker caps.
Code: 1044060002
1⅜ in salt shaker caps.
Code: 1044060001
Salt & pepper shaker containers.
Code: 050-7050
1 in bungs. Code: 1044050001

Chefwarekits
www.chefwarekits.com
267-888-6216
Silicone sealing rings. Code 47281

Packard Woodworks Inc.
www.packardwoodworks.com
Tel. 1-800-683-8876
¾ in salt shaker caps. Code: 154004
1 in Red rubber bung. Code: 151019
1 in White rubber bung.
Code: 151019-W

Rockler Woodworking
www.rockler.com
Tel. 1-800-279-4441
White synthetic finishing pads.
Code: 93477
Salt & pepper shaker containers.
Code: 43535
1⅜ in salt shaker caps.
Code: 48148

Chasingbutterfliesboutique.
Ebay seller
www.ebay.com
Search word string : *Salt & pepper pot bung*
¾ in & 1 in rubber bungs

Lee Valley Tools Ltd
www.leevalley.com
Tel. (from USA) 1-800-871-8158
(from Canada) 1-800-267-8767
Salt & pepper shaker containers.
Code: 88K81.58

Amazon.com
www.amazon.com
Polycarbonate Tubing, 1 in ID x 1¼ in OD x ⅛ in Wall, Clear Color 24 in L
From: Small Parts
Part Number: TPC-125/20

Acknowledgments

Project 19, the Pestle and Mortar, was designed by Ian Woodford.

It is included here in the book with his permission and my thanks.

My thanks go to Rita Mitchell (who has a photographic studio like no other) for taking so many great photographs that have been included in this book.

My thanks also go to Ian Woodford who had the necessary equipment and knowledge to take a number of the excellent photographs used in the book.
Jim and Andrea Blaho from Artisan Ideas did a great job editing the book.

Marc and Linda Erthein from Vermont have been good enough to proof read the book. Marc with his woodturning head on and Linda used with her vast editing skills ensured that this Limey had got it right.

Thanks to Ian Holdsworth for spending his time going through the book with the fine-tooth comb he still uses.

And thanks to the book's very talented graphic designer, Elisabeth Forster, and to Daniela Rossato for the layout.

Picture Credits:
Ian Woodford, pages 6-8, 12-14, 18-20, 26-28, 30, 42, 44, 46, 48 & 62
Rita Mitchell, pages 1, 3, 16, 26, 30, 32, 34, 36, 38, 40, 46, 50, 52, 54, 56, 60, 62, 63-65 & 68
Chris West, pages 15, 17, 20-23, 32, 36, 42 & 48
Line drawings are by Chris West.

ABOUT THE AUTHOR

Chris has been enjoying his craft for over 35 years. During the last dozen or so Chris has specialized in designing and turning salt and pepper mills and shakers.

His career began in the computer industry.
- He started out by serving a five year apprenticeship as an electro-mechanical engineer.
Yes, computers did have moving parts in those days! One important aspect of that work was the necessity of working within tight tolerances. This gave Chris the necessary skills for turning matching pairs of shakers.

After taking early retirement he now spends a good deal of his time in his workshop.

Chris's schedule also includes taking his wood-turning experience to 'outside' groups by giving talks to interested social organizations.

Many of Chris's shakers have appeared in the UK's *Woodturning magazine*. He feels that through this book he can share his knowledge and experience with many woodturners, budding and experienced alike.

He is also an active member of the Hampshire Woodturners Association, the Test Valley Woodturners and an international member of the American Association of Woodturners (AAW).